When a young boy turns up on Janet's doorstep in small town Oregon, little does she know how much she will come to treasure him. Comical remembrances of her **own** childhood add seasoning to this haunting book. If you have experienced dark nights of the soul and choose to look fearlessly at life's shadows, follow along with wisdom keeper Janet Richards as your guide.

**Keddy Ann Outlaw**

With both eloquence and a perceptive curiosity, Janet Richards examines the potency of random encounters that can impact a life. Boldly going where she does not want to be, the author focuses both on America's complex medical struggles and her own spiritual and philosophical quandaries as she faces the potential early death for her young beloved friend. Her book made me look in my own shadow areas, which I prefer to ignore. A great page-turner. We can all learn from it.

**Mary Ann Reese**
**Journalist and Author**

Janet Richards has given Monty the invaluable gift of immortality. She shows his indomitable ability to say "yes" to life even when forces are conspiring to defeat him. But one force is on his side and that is the force of love. That love diminishes the differences in age and lifestyle and blesses not only the two protagonists but also the reader of this wonderful book. Monty's spirit lives on.

**Ruth Ann Brown**

Whatever your perspective on life you will want this true tome to end differently. But it can't. It is written by a truthsayer. Come to this story of uncomfortable darkness faulted by lovely light.

**Dan'l Markum**
**Author of *Contagious Love***

I found this book to be a compelling and powerful meditation on a young man's brief life, faith, and the problem of pain. I knew Monty as a child and remember when I stopped by Janet's house and found Monty and her dressed in black super hero caps flitting about the house. This image has stuck with me.

**Pat Patla**

Janet Richards wrote Monty's story as a promise to his family and to him. He changed her life, and he will have an impact on you, the reader, too. Morrie Schwartz, who died from Lou Gehrig's disease, was quoted as saying: *"The most important thing in life is to learn how to give out of love and let it in."* Regardless of what happened to Monty, he often responded with a thumbs up. The reader will feel like giving the same response after reading this most poignant story.

**Sister Margaret Johnson**

Janet Richards tells the true story of a remarkable young man and his battle with cancer. The tenderness she finds in the harshest of moments is both cathartic and refreshing. As a mom who has walked similar halls of suffering with a beloved son, I thank Janet for reminding us that God directs our lives, even in times of pain.

**Pam Thorson**
**Author of *Out of the Shadows* &**
***Song in the Night***

# Only a Shadow

## JANET RICHARDS

WestBow Press
A DIVISION OF THOMAS NELSON
& ZONDERVAN

Copyright © 2018 Janet Richards.

All rights reserved. No part of this book may be used or reproduced by any means, graphic, electronic, or mechanical, including photocopying, recording, taping or by any information storage retrieval system without the written permission of the author except in the case of brief quotations embodied in critical articles and reviews.

This book is a work of non-fiction. Unless otherwise noted, the author and the publisher make no explicit guarantees as to the accuracy of the information contained in this book and in some cases, names of people and places have been altered to protect their privacy.

WestBow Press books may be ordered through booksellers or by contacting:

WestBow Press
A Division of Thomas Nelson & Zondervan
1663 Liberty Drive
Bloomington, IN 47403
www.westbowpress.com
1 (866) 928-1240

Because of the dynamic nature of the Internet, any web addresses or links contained in this book may have changed since publication and may no longer be valid. The views expressed in this work are solely those of the author and do not necessarily reflect the views of the publisher, and the publisher hereby disclaims any responsibility for them.

Any people depicted in stock imagery provided by Getty Images are models, and such images are being used for illustrative purposes only. Certain stock imagery © Getty Images.

Scripture quotations taken from the New American Standard Bible® (NASB), Copyright © 1960, 1962, 1963, 1968, 1971, 1972, 1973, 1975, 1977, 1995 by The Lockman Foundation Used by permission. www.Lockman.org

ISBN: 978-1-9736-2398-4 (sc)
ISBN: 978-1-9736-2399-1 (e)

Library of Congress Control Number: 2018903700

Print information available on the last page.

WestBow Press rev. date: 06/14/2018

*"What if earth
Be but the shadow of heaven and things there in
Each to other life, more than on earth is thought."*

— Milton's Paradise Lost

# Chapter 1

Every story has a beginning. Every relationship starts with a moment and a meeting. Though an untold number of encounters occur in a lifetime, seldom do any of us know the power of their impact in passing. Swept up in the business of living, enticed and mesmerized by the sirens of the world tempting us to ego, scandal, and pleasure, it's easy to overlook the potential of a single point in time and all the golden magic it can hold. The world spins on, gracing every human on the planet with its offerings, and so few we embrace.

But there are specific scenes that stick with a person – the firsts and lasts, the glorious triumphs, crushing losses, and the endings and beginnings that punctuate life. This story starts with one of those snapshots – a single frame captured on the fly in a glance out of the driver's side window of my Aerostar van on an Indian summer day in early October. I've just pulled to the curb in front my house in Lakeview, Oregon after a quick trip to Safeway on my lunch hour. The sixth period bell at the middle school where I work is about to ring. I'm on a mission.

I'll never know why I decided to park in front of my house at that particular time of day in 2001, or what possessed me to run to the grocery store during my lunch break in the first place. I always drove the family car into the driveway off the alley behind our house, never out front. On a typical weekday during the school year I would be eating a yogurt in the staff room, crafting lesson plans at my desk, or checking out books for sixth graders on recess. I rarely, if ever, left school during working hours unless required to chaperone a bonus activity at the Alger Theatre downtown or evacuate the building during a fire drill.

And what am I doing in this frontier community of less than 3,000 in the eastern Oregon desert? It certainly isn't my idea of an ideal place to live. I'm a native New Yorker from Queens, an urbanite who thrives on access to eclectic diversity, ethnic restaurants, artsy shops, and the rich cultural experiences that a metropolitan environment has to offer. Tumbling weeds, rowdy rodeos, and cow pie kickin' cowboys roaming the range on horseback are the stuff of Zane Grey novels and episodes of Bonanza, not fodder for my dreams.

One hundred miles of tumbleweed and juniper stretch between what's affectionately called the "Tallest Town in Oregon" (elevation 4,801) and a city of any size. Long fanny-numbing car rides to sporting events, school concerts, and medical appointments are a given for every person who takes up residence in this remote enclave. There's no bus out of this old cattle town, at least not since the stagecoach transport service with two passenger seats shut down. The nearest Costco is a seven hour round trip, and, if you are craving a Big Mac, you can count on four. A single Safeway is currently the only grocery serving the entire county which is geographically larger than the state of Connecticut.

My body and spirit wilted in protest when my husband drove our family into L-town in the fall of 1989. The arid landscape at the foot of the Warner Mountains was as disheartening as the scent of sunbaked sagebrush, the whirling dust devils that circled our car, and the swarms of kamikaze locust obliterating our windshield with a thick yellow goo. I failed to see anything positive about exile to this isolated place and saw myself aging before my time, every opportunity vaporizing, and all hopes for a good life becoming as parched and dry as the miles and miles of dusty road leading in and out of nowhere. But my husband's desire to practice rural medicine could not be denied despite these obvious drawbacks. Lakeview became my destiny, and, on the day in question in 2001 and I've been living there for over a decade.

This is where I have been planted, and here I sit in a van in front of our new two story house in the Oregon Outback. I glance across the street as the vehicle rolls to a stop. A small blonde boy and a woman who looks just like him are sitting side by side in child-size chairs next to a small wooden table on the sidewalk in front of their dilapidated rental home. A pitcher and a stack of paper cups rest on the table which has a homemade sign taped to its side. The kid and his mother are selling lemonade.

The family moved into the aged rental directly across from us months ago, but somehow their presence failed to register. Our family lives in a new house with a wraparound porch, built on a double lot in the center of town which looks out of place amidst all the two-bedroom dwellings with asbestos shingles and carports that surrounded it. This conglomeration of housing options illustrates the unique homogeny of the population of Lakeview. Because the town is hemmed in by mountains to the east, a huge sewer pond to the west, and highway 395 running north to south, there's not much room to expand. Lovely split levels and pristine ranch-style homes with groomed lawns sit next to tiny bungalows and crumbling cracker boxes nestled in the weeds in this strip of a community. That's L-town.

Perhaps it's not surprising that we haven't met our new neighbors despite the intimacy of small town living. It's easy to rest in the swirling eddies of our prosaic lives and fail to notice the people and events that surround us even in a place as tiny and isolated as L-town. The population of this remote berg includes a diverse mix of ranchers and townies, government employees, relocated professionals, and those that were born here and never left. Natives and recent transplants often don't mix. People travel in different circles, settle into comfy cliques, and socialize with family and a circumscribed group of friends. It's like that everywhere but more obvious in places where the options for relationship and recreation are so limited.

The boy and his mother stare at me as I pour out of my vehicle and scramble around to passenger side to retrieve my purchases. I feel their gaze as I trudge toward the front door carrying a jug of milk and a paper sack of groceries destined for the refrigerator. *I'll run over to say hello and buy some lemonade once I put the food away,* I tell myself, as thoughts of the tasks that lie ahead for the afternoon and evening vie for attention. We're planning to go to my teenage daughter's basketball game at four, and there's a video I need to set up for the next two periods at school. I'm wondering what to make for dinner. Minutes later I scurry out the front door, coins in hand. The stand has disappeared. I've lost my chance. The proprietors shut down business for the day and moved inside.

Over the years I've imagined and reimagined that young mother and her freckled, tow-headed boy just as they were on that sunny fall afternoon in 2001, snuggled close at a small table in front of their home with a frosty jug of lemonade hoping for customers. The image brings to mind memories of my own children setting up shop under the trees on the corner by our house in St. Maries, Idaho. They're calling out to potential patrons in their cars, accosting every pedestrian within a two block radius, splashing sugary Kool-Aid into waxed cups, their lips and tee-shirts stained purple from frequent samplings of their product. My son clutches a *Ziplock* bag full of dimes, sticky from counting, and my daughter shouts the latest tally to me as I watch from an open kitchen window. I'm their mother and I love them more than I can say. Their joy is mine.

I think of that beautiful woman, her eyes following me, a small-town physician's wife, trucking to front door of my fancy home with nary a nod or a word. I know nothing of this mother's reality, her past, her dreams, or her sufferings – even now I know almost nothing. Yet her love for her small son rushes across the physical space and the social constraints that divide us. Her life touches mine. I will never be the same.

Sometimes it seems as if I've floated through life like a leaf on a stream – the days washing over only to slip away as I bobble on a current that impels me where it wants me to go. So many decisions are made on a whim, without serious reflection or reasoned thought. Should I run to the store now or wait till after the game? Is there time to listen to my neighbor recount the details of her recent car accident, or would it be better to mop the kitchen floor before dinner? Should I stop to chat with an elderly friend downtown or get back to school and finish some paperwork? Too often selfish motives prevail. Too often the current moves me along the path of least resistance.

How seldom I consider the ramifications of my flippant choices – the good, the bad, the so-called "sins" of commission or omission – or the mysterious way they might play out during my brief sojourn on this horizontal plane and beyond to eternity. A pat on the back, a kind or hurtful word or gesture, or even sacrificing a few minutes to lend an ear might ripple through time, infinitely affecting legions of people known and unknown, born and unborn.

Was that specific scene at that specific time of day something that was in some mysterious way meant to happen? Could the impulse to park in a different spot or the decision to wait until after school to shop for food have changed everything? Is it possible that something as simple as taking the time to buy a cool drink at a child's stand or raising an arm to offer a friendly wave might carry weight that echoes through eternity?

My husband and I notice an ambulance parked by the house across from us as we are returning from a walk up the canyon the next afternoon. The terrible news makes its way to us through the small town grapevine. The woman I happened to see sitting at the lemonade stand with her boy on that ordinary Thursday is the mother of three children. Her name is Heather Kay Hossick.

And she's dead at the age of thirty-three— a victim of suicide

# Chapter 2

Information travels like flames through dry stubble in a town like Lakeview. One spark, a single telling of a news-worthy story, can set the whole community ablaze. It doesn't matter if the individuals involved are tiny minnows or big fish in this little pond – everyone knows at least one person touched by the latest dispatch, and people talk.

Residents in close-knit communities want to be in the know when it comes to the latest grist to hit the mill, and rumors fly on every whiff of high desert air often spinning into bizarre versions of the truth in the process. An elderly woman's fainting spell in front of the courthouse develops into a vivid account of a drive-by shooting. A yellow lab on the grammar school lawn becomes a cougar. Small town prattle morphs in strange ways more often than not taking on new details with each telling until the original account no longer bears any resemblance to the truth.

It wasn't long before everyone in town became aware of the circumstances of Heather's death and the tragedy it was for her husband and children. Conjectures about the reason for her suicide circulated – a recurrence of breast cancer, struggles with relationships, and unbearable despair over the past that reached a breaking point were just a few of the explanations that made the circuit. Of course none of the stories could be verified. The truth died with Heather.

Someone in a beauty salon once noted that "gossip is a form of prayer," and as soon as L-town folk start praying together news spreads like feathers in a windstorm. Hugs, hot dishes, and helping hands appear out of nowhere.

Love lands where it's wanted and needed and even where it's not. People gave of their time and talents to support a family whose son was killed in a bicycle accident and also reached out to the driver whose car hit the boy. Every congregation in Lakeview participated in organizing a dinner to benefit for a high school sophomore diagnosed with bone cancer. Teenage waiters wore white dress shirts for the event, and Fetch's, the local men's clothing store, was soon out of stock. A recipe from *Bon Appetite* made the rounds, and twenty-two raspberry cheesecakes appeared overnight. As is so often the case in small communities, like Lakeview, residents collectively grieve when one of their own goes down, and they do what they can to help.

Lakeview retains some of the endearing elements of a time when people lived in small agrarian bergs and stayed there. It holds traces of the era when relationships with townsfolk were central to the quality of a person's day-to-day existence. Movies often glorify these Mayberry-style environments where people know their neighbors and feel accepted in spite of their flaws, failings, and Barney Fife-like foibles. A hunger for this spirit of kinship explains the popularity of television shows like *The Office* and *Friends*, even in reruns, and why viewers return year after year to watch *It's a Wonderful Life*. We crave the vicarious experience of a type intimate community lifestyle that's quickly vanishing.

It's common knowledge that the L-town mayor tipples now and then, and that the dog catcher despises dogs. People accept and love the jolly librarian at the public library who can't contain her obsession with books on quilting (the small library's inventory includes hundreds), even though she falls asleep at her desk behind the check-out counter every afternoon after ingesting a gargantuan lunch special at the Indian Village Café. Everyone expects to see roly poly Mr. Eri, dressed in his too-short high-waisted polyester pants held up by suspenders, sitting in a plastic lawn chair outside his variety store on Main Street. He's always there after school gets out in June, stopping customers as they walk by to catch up on the latest scuttlebutt wafting through town on a summer breeze. Most townsfolk know when to avoid a visit to the DMV because the only clerk on duty is a stickler for the rules and never fails to flip a closed sign at exactly 10, 12, and 2 on the dot in order to take his half-hour breaks, mid-transaction if necessary, no matter how many people are waiting.

These citizens, with all their quirks and idiosyncrasies, are simply accepted for their unique, frequently eccentric contributions to the patchwork fabric of community diversity. Socioeconomic circumstances and varying lifestyles may be obvious but rarely hold much sway when daily existence requires frequent interaction, cooperation, and a drive for the common good. The dentist pulls his car over to inquire if your son is wearing his retainer. The school bus driver calls you at home when your dog escapes the yard and is wandering on the lawn of the courthouse. And when a teenager returns to class two days after his mother's death from suicide the principal notices.

And so it was on the Monday morning following Heather's death that my boss at Daly Middle School, Will Cahill, brought a teenage boy, a John Cusack look-alike with sad eyes, into the library for a few days away from inquisitive peers. His name is Daniel and he is Heather's oldest son.

One of the advantages of the elective class I taught for high school students was the chance it provided for kids to interface with the instructor while gaining work experience and computer skills. Library aides, as these students were called, were responsible for the daily tasks involved in operating a middle school library. They viewed movie clips on how to create a resume and ace an interview and published a weekly homeroom newsletter comprised of edifying stories, which often lead to interesting philosophical discussions. Students also listened to a wide variety of music genres while they worked – Bob Dylan, Jimmy Hendrix, and *Korn* to name a few – and had a chance to discuss the lyrics of different popular songs. Heather's boy proved to be intelligent and hard-working, and I was pleased that he fit right in with the other high school students in the program. Daniel spent his days checking books in and out of the library and participating in class discussions and programs.

We were strangers at first, but after four full days together a certain level of trust developed. I baked the cake that I usually deliver to families who have lost loved ones, a Bountiful Bundt Ring, and carried it to the mortuary where friends and relatives gathered on Wednesday evening for Heather's wake. He invited me to his mother's memorial service at the end of the week.

This is how it all began: A fluke trip to Safeway at noon on an ordinary Thursday, a principal's tender heart, a *Bundt* cake, and a young boy's invitation to his mother's funeral, all came together.

The stars aligned and the pieces of this story began to fall into place as if choreographed on high.

# Chapter 3

> *"They say you die twice. One time when you stop breathing and a second time, a bit later on, when somebody says your name for the last time."*
>
> — Banksy

The family scheduled a memorial service for Heather for 11 a.m. on Friday at the First Baptist Church, Reverend Richard Bryson officiating. It was rumored that Heather was not a religious woman, but most townsfolk were satisfied to let God be the judge of that.

A house of worship can be a haven, a quiet space away from the noise of the world and a good place to say goodbye.

I arrive at the church early. It's a bright morning and my eyes squint to adjust to the dusky light in the narthex as I open the heavy front doors and step inside. Lakeview's Baptist venue offers everything one would expect to find at a Protestant church in small town America – classic steeple, pillared entry, smoky candlelit interior, and plain cross on the wall behind a wooden lectern. Daniel, his stepdad, and a few other family members crouch in the front row, but Heather's other children are nowhere in sight. Several small groups of mourners are scattered in the pews but no one I know. Heather didn't live in Lakeview very long, and we traveled in different circles. I'm here because Daniel invited me.

I slide onto a wooden bench in the back and sit to collect my thoughts. The shock of sudden death and the pain of knowing this death was by choice can't be denied. The air is heavy with unspoken sadness. No one's moving or talking.

Most Lake County residents have attended funerals in this particular church, some packed to the rafters with mourners and enough floral arrangements to stock every flower shop within a hundred mile radius. Services for prominent citizens sometimes include dramatic performances —scores of doves set free from the front steps, butterflies released from tiny cardboard prisons, or bouquets of balloons for a similar effect to symbolize the dead person's assent to heaven and reunion with their God. Musical tributes by Lakeview's much beloved piano teacher, Mrs. Lynch and/or local choirs are common, especially when the deceased is well-known. A typical Oregon Outback funeral might feature an old cowhand reciting cowboy poetry for a fallen rancher, or a vocal soloist who personally knew and loved the departed soul, offering heartfelt renditions of the deceased person's favorite hymns. Hour long slide shows and/or videos chronicling every details of a Lake County resident's time on earth, lengthy eulogies by family members and friends, and sumptuous after service buffet luncheons are expected. The proceedings are sometimes piped into adjoining rooms on portable televisions to accommodate the masses.

But there are no crowds here, and there will be no live music or pageantry. A country song streams from a boom box on the carpeted stairs to the altar. The music dissipates into the almost empty room and sounds as if it's coming from some place far away. Two over-sized sprays of irises, a common choice for funerals, stand alone on the altar to announce the reason for the gathering. These and altar candles emitting gentle light are the only decorations of note. Small clusters of mourners huddle together on hard polished oak seats waiting for things to begin. A few hustle up the stairs to the choir loft in back as the preacher steps to the pulpit to offer a prayer. Heather's service is a simple prototype of the Desert Rose Funeral Chapel's generic memorial ceremony on the no-frills plan.

Pastor Bryson takes advantage of the obituary published in the local Lakeview County Examiner to summarize Heather's short life. He admits that he didn't know the young mother, and that they never met. He recites a second-hand anecdote or two, followed by the customary twenty-third psalm. The minister is kind and sincere and gives his standard, impassioned sermon on the resurrection and Jesus's victory over death to a sullen, captive audience. Without missing a beat he grabs a portable mic resting on the ambo and calls for mourners to share their memories.

A gentleman dressed in jeans and a tee-shirt stands to express his condolences in a single sentence.

"I hope the woman's in a better place."

The man crumples into his seat and everyone looks around. There is no one to take his place.

A hush falls over the congregants – an uncomfortable stillness drops out of nowhere like a velvet pall gently draped over a casket. The minister freezes like one of those human statues at the Venetian Casino in Las Vegas, his arm extended, mic in hand, scanning the mute congregants, eyes wide with hope, face pale. Pastor Bryson repeats his offer and waits for one minute that stretches into two, and then begins to pace. The opportunity for people to pay tribute to Heather is slipping away. No one is moving. The unexpected pause pulses with pain. I take a deep breath, hoping that someone will step up.

Who am I? ...a lousy neighbor, mindlessly living a middle-class life in security and comfort – too busy to take the time to welcome neighborhood newcomers or stop for a few moments to buy lemonade from a child. I know next to nothing about Heather. I only saw her once and then only for a few seconds. We never spoke. And yet I rise from the pew and hear words come from my mouth as if from somewhere beyond my conscious will.

"Heather lived across the street from me. I saw her sitting at a lemonade stand in front of her house with her youngest child at noon. Although we never met, I've had the chance to spend some time with Heather's oldest son, Daniel. He is a good boy, and I know that Heather loved her children."

I am the last in the assembly to speak. The minister brings the service to a hasty close with a brief prayer, a salutation, and an "Amen." Mourners stand and scatter like marbles dumped onto on a granite floor. It's over.

There's no aroma of fresh perked coffee wafting from the church dining hall or fancy cake reception to follow. No lavish luncheon spread featuring honey-baked ham, *au gratin* potatoes, and buttery rolls with homemade jam set out by the grey-haired church ladies, or even a chance to hug or cry with family members and reminisce about Heather's life. A few drive to Sunset Park Cemetery for the burial. Most race for home.

And I scurry too, unaware that someone is watching me from the balcony. That small boy I saw sitting with his mother days earlier is up in the choir loft.

His name is Monty Martin McDonald, and he is about to change my life.

# Chapter 4

*"Whoever receives a little child like this in
my name receives Me."*

— Matthew 18: 5

It's about three o'clock, several hours after Heather's funeral service, and I'm in the process of mixing the batter for another one of my *Bundt* cakes because that's what I usually do on Fridays. The doorbell rings, and I rinse and dry my hands before running to answer. There's a child standing on our front porch – a very blonde boy of about eight with a slight build and a lot of freckles. He's dressed in a white dress shirt and khaki pants, and wearing wire-rimmed glasses. It's the lemonade salesman and he looks up at me as I stand in the doorway.

"Hi, I'm Monty. I just wanted to come over to say hi. I live across the street."

"Well hello, Monty. I'm Mrs. Richards. It's nice to meet you."

"I saw you bringing a cake."

"I'm so sorry about your mom Monty. Did you get to taste the cake? Was it any good?""

"I think so. I didn't try it."

15

The young lad squirms and looks around as if trying to think of something to say.

"I saw you at the church too."

"I was there. Your brother invited me to your mother's memorial service. I know Daniel from school."

"We just got back from the cemetery."

A lump forms in my throat. He's so small and *so* young. I'm stunned by his courage and vulnerability and awed by the moxie it took to come over to my house. For a moment I am speechless.

"Would you like to help me finish picking up stuff in the garden out back Monty? I bet we can find some treasures out there, and I could really use your help."

"Yeah, and do you have any pets Mrs. Richards? I really like animals. I have a cat."

"Yes Monty, we have a dog. Let's go meet her."

Monty and I head for the backyard and spend the rest of the fall afternoon in the garden digging up tiny bifurcated carrots and harvesting shriveled cherry tomatoes off the crisp stalks in my husband's vegetable patch. We use toothpicks to assemble our gleanings into figures and soon have a row of miniature men and women with tomato heads, pea pod torsos, and carrot legs sitting on the railing of the front porch. Our black lab, Pneuma, runs to and fro in the yard and she and Monty become instant friends.

In time I learn that Monty is not an orphan. He and his two siblings continue to live with their stepdad, Rick, in the house across the street. Rick is an affable man with a ready smile. Although he rarely acknowledges my relationship with Monty, I eventually come to know him well enough for an occasional polite greeting on the street. Heather's first husband. and the father of her three children is another story. He always seems glad to see me.

Boone, as the children's dad is called, lives in town and is still part of the kid's lives. He's employed doing odd jobs at an old resort at the edge of town. We meet by chance one day when

Monty and I drive out to Hunter's Hot Spring Motel to feed the ducks, watch Lakeview's famous geyser, and throw stones in the pond. Monty is excited and runs toward him. Boone's eyes shine when he sees his boy approaching, and he greets him with open arms. Monty falls into them. Boone can't hide his love.

The weeks and months and then years after that day when Monty and I first met on the porch meld together into a blurry collage. Monty stops by after school most days, but I never know for sure when he'll show. It isn't long before he foregoes the formality of ringing the doorbell and just lets himself in. The school where I work is only a block from my house and I'm usually home by 3:30 and available to listen. Monty likes to talk.

Sometimes we do things together – run to Polar Bear for a soft cone, walk to the library, or head out for an impromptu stroll around town, but most of the time we just chat about school and things at home. Even though he's only eight, Monty has the verbal skills of someone much older and the ability to sound like a credible authority on any subject that arises. He also tells fantastic stories, adamantly defending their veracity despite evidence to the contrary, which is a habit that annoys and even angers some of the people in his circle.

"Have you heard of goat suckers, Mrs. Richards? They're these giant lizards, as big as a bobcat, with sharp spikes down the back. They can fly and suck the blood out of animals like goats and sheep. They're vampires."

"I don't know, Monty. I've never heard of such a thing."

"A science experiment in a lab went wrong and somehow they got loose."

"That sounds like science fiction, Monty. That can't be true."

"They have these weird eyes that glow in the dark, like aliens, and they can suck three times their own weight in blood."

"I'd hate to be the poor goat that runs into one of those!" I tell him, hoping he'll change the subject. My youngest daughter later admonishes me for letting Monty get away with too much.

"Giant flying lizards as big as cougars Mom? Sucking three times their own weight in blood! You wouldn't let me get away with the things that boy says and does."

Right away I understand that arguing with Monty is a losing battle. He's immensely creative and tenacious to a fault. His confabulated tales are always over the top and full of questionable material that can't be verified, but, for some reason, they don't annoy me. In fact they're entertaining, and I find that I enjoy his inventive phrasing and amazing vocabulary.

My kids are grown, two already off to college, so we don't have a stash of toys, but we do have costumes stored in the attic, and Monty uses them to turn our dog into a princess, a flower in a pot, and a wizard. He constructs forts using afghans and the end tables and chairs in our family room and crafts inventions out of things lying around the house. I quickly discover that inventing is one of his passions and help him collect the necessary cardboard tubes, rubber bands, and other supplies he needs to make a periscope, an elaborate candy dispenser, and a working flashlight from instructions he found in a library book.

"He makes such a mess in the house, Mom," my teenage daughter complains, and there's no doubt about that. His visits do generate a fair amount of household clutter, but I cut him more slack than I did for my own three kids at that age.

"There seems no harm in providing a space where he can be himself," I tell Noelle. "He doesn't come over every afternoon. He's been through a lot."

The easy days are when we head outside. Monty loves the natural world, and he's always up for an outing whether it be a church picnic or a walk around town. He brings injured birds and animals to our house for medical attention and talks incessantly about his cat. Sometimes we walk along the gravel alleys behind our house flinging birdseed from paper cups to the bevies of quail that make their home there while belting out the song from *Mary Poppins*..."Feed the birds, tuppence a bag, tuppence, tuppence,

tuppence a bag." We toss handfuls of seed to the wind and racing each other back to the garage to refill our cups.

Some days he just helps me cook, standing at the counter on a chair, watching me cut vegetables and meat, and helping me stir a sauce or mix a cake batter. More often than not, he heads straight for the dog bed in the corner of our family room where our black lab waits ready to offer therapy without conditions. I watch as he lays there, eyes closed behind smudged spectacles, forearms crossed in perfect repose, enveloped in a canine embrace. He's smiling and the sight of his peace brings me peace as well.

Who can look into the eyes of a newborn or a very young baby and not be moved? Their tiny orbs are clear, deep, and full of wonder as they look up and out with perfect innocence, melting into the arms of their loving caregivers. Babies put everything in their mouths as if driven to consume the world, to taste its bounty and make it their own. They are guileless. The eyes of each one of my grandchildren sparkle with purity and trust. They are unaware of all the hardship and heartache that life can hold.

Not so for children of trauma. Not so. The ones, like Monty, who have lost a parent in a sudden, violent way live in an environment that's ever in flux. Perhaps adults don't always do what they say they will do, or no one's home to set parameters or provide a safe haven, a Band-Aid, or a hug. Grownups have to make a living, and they have their own struggles. Siblings can't replace a mother. They are hurting too.

Something unthinkable has happened to this young child and his brother and sister through no fault of their own. The absence of reassuring routines, solid expectations, and stability, along with the memories and loss, add to an unsettling sense that world is scary, and things might fall apart at any time, in any place, and without warning. Sometimes there's nowhere or no one to turn to, nothing to insure that another disaster won't blow. The grating whirl of a garbage disposal, sudden roar of a passing semi, or a car backing firing can feel like raw pain to a youngster who is ever alert, waiting for the next hit. It's hard to listen and concentrate at school, and the teachers complain. Even though the staff members know about the tragedy, they can't excuse bad behavior. Maybe Ritalin is the answer. At least that might be worth a try.

Early on I realize that Monty is a remarkable person. It's not just his precocious verbosity or his imagination; it's his extraordinary resilience and amazing ability to access the resources he needs that were so evident from the first day he came over to our house. He takes it upon self to walk to evening meetings of the Awana Program at the Baptist Church and to the library to check out books for his inventive creations. He's sharp and uses our computer to looks up how to file for a patent, treat a cat that has ringworm, or provide good nutrition for an ailing sparrow. He's fond of quoting common adages and seems to be trying to make sense of what he sees and experiences in an effort to find justice and order in a world that is full of chaos.

"Two wrongs don't make a right, Mrs. Richards," he tells me one day after complaining about being grounded by his stepdad.

"I'm not sure how that saying applies to your situation, Monty."

"Rick says I'm grounded for a month, and I didn't do anything."

"You must have done something."

"Yeah, but not something worth being grounded for a month. That's just wrong. Two wrongs don't make a right."

Monty often uses trite aphorisms to get a handle on what's happening in his world. This would later be evident in his affinity for the morality tales of *My Little Pony* cartoons and reality television programs about law and order. When life spins out of control, solid statements of some sort of truth are something to hold onto. He could also be funny.

"Life gives you lemons, make lemonade, Mrs. Richards"

he tells me when I start complaining about rotten avocados I'd purchased at the local Safeway.

"Or you make guacamole."

One special afternoon about a year after we met, we walk downtown to Eri's Variety Store to buy a votive candle. It soon becomes our "candle of forgiveness" and finds a home on my kitchen counter inside a square cube of clear glass. On one snowy Saturday in February, Monty and I conduct a short ceremony of lighting the candle and talking about good times Monty remembers with his mother. We later decide to jump in the car to visit her grave. It takes some time to locate Heather's plaque among numerous others covered with snow, but, once we find it, Monty and I kneel to scrape it clear with bear hands. We cry. Lighting the candle of forgiveness becomes part of our after-school routine every day after that.

Months later the glass holder fractures down the middle into two solid halves. Monty and I shove the pieces together, insert a fresh votive in its little metal pan and light the wick. Over time many tiny candles burn themselves away while the two of us stand over them bathed in their light.

"Cracks are good," I tell Monty, remembering a song from the library aide class.

Leonard Cohen says "That's how the light gets in."

Monty smiles at me.

Corny aphorisms float his boat.

Monty moved to the Key Peninsula to live with Boone at his Grandma Yvonne's house in Home, Washington when he turned eleven. Not long after that my husband and I left Lakeview, too, and bought a house in Moscow, Idaho.

Monty and I continued to make an effort to stay in touch across the miles. I remembered his birthday every June and send post cards during our vacations at Joni and Friends Family Camp in California every summer. It was fun to surprise him with wacky Christmas presents – a box of novelty gum and candies from *World Market* in the shape of various foods and household doodads, an electronic inventors set, and a big box of paperbacks including the entire Brian Jacques *Redwall* series, which Monty told me he was into reading at the time. Monty sends me gifts too: a set of plastic food containers in a spinning rack that he ordered from *Home Shopping Club*, a picture frame, and some of his drawings – one of a horse and one of a Christian cross.

When the boy turned twelve, I drove to the Key Peninsula to visit him, and we took a hike along the Purdy slough and stopped at Lulu's diner to enjoy a leisurely lunch with his grandma and Boone's wife, Lisa. Neither Monty nor I cared to talk on the phone much, but we did manage to call each other once in a while, his voice growing deeper with each passing year.

"I took myself off Ritalin Mrs. Richards," he told me during one of our phone conversations. "I just stopped it the day after I turned fourteen. I never needed that medication. It was messing with me."

He was calling from a travel trailer that Boone fixed for him in his grandma's yard.

"I'm sitting in it right now, Mrs. Richards. My dad rigged it so I have a power source coming from the house, so I can read at night and have my own space."

One day he confided that he was having trouble at school.

"Yeah, it's not easy when you don't fit in, Mrs. Richards. And believe me I *don't* fit in. I really *don't* fit in."

And as always, he had a lot to say about his animals.

Monty sent me a postcard when he was fourteen which I still have.

*I thought I might send this to you because I have not written to you for a long time. I got a new cat named Fluffy, and she is a very well trained cat. She mainly sleeps all day. Bye*

*Only a Shadow*

As much as we shared after school during those three years after Heather's death, I know very little about Monty's life after he left Lakeview. I only saw him once after that and then for only a few hours.

But everything would change on February 21, 2013. Perhaps it was written in the stars.

On that day our paths would cross again

## Chapter 5

*"Life is always on the edge of death; narrow streets lead to the same place as wide avenues, and a little candle burns itself out just like a flaming torch does. I choose my own way to burn."*

— Sophie Scholl
German student and anti-Nazi
Political activist executed by the Nazis

As much as we like to think that we are in control of destiny, able to craft our own journey, and create our own authentic lives, there are things that happen in life that will change our carefully crafted plans. I think of a friend who suffered a life altering brain injury when a light fixture fell on her head while she was shopping at the local A&P, or the parents of children with autism who never knew that they were signing up to be caregivers 24-hours a day, seven days a week, for the rest of their lives when they opted to become parents. I'm reminded of a teenage boy who became a quadriplegic wrestling with his Dad, and my friend Christina, who was diagnosed with multiple sclerosis at the age of nine. Even job opportunities, serendipitous meetings and second chances can appear, through no effort or choice on our part, to send us to new places, exciting adventures and experiences beyond our ability to imagine. "Stuff happens" is the sanitized version of a common adage. Itineraries change and so must our expectations.

If the goal of a truly meaningful existence is selfless self-donation – to lose our lives for the sake of others as Jesus did, or to seek greatness in servant-hood as Martin Luther King suggested – most would prefer to select incremental offerings of the less painful sort (ie) periodic donations to a favorite charity, a stint volunteering at a local soup kitchen, or a week-long mission trip to build houses in Central America as a way to see the country while serving the poor. These altruistic endeavors might suffice. No one wants sacrifice by being speared to death, which was the fate of Eliot and Fleming, who were preaching to the indigenous people in the jungles of Ecuador, or death by decapitation like Sophie Scholl experienced in her demonstration of immense bravery in the face of Nazi evil. No one *chooses* to face insurmountable odds in order to be an example of courage and inspiration for others. No one chooses cancer.

A serious illness didn't cross my mind on that day in February when I ran across a post on *Facebook* from Monty's sister, Christine:

*Wishing my baby brother lots of courage and strength as he begins this terrible journey he has no choice in not fighting.*

The last time I talked to Monty, he was excited about finally finishing his GED and getting ready for his high school prom. Was he accused of a crime and facing jail time or worse? Did he drink and drive? Sell drugs? As a third grader he'd been caught stealing from the till at the town pool and spent some time in counseling with the Lakeview Police Department, but, as far as I knew, he had no other run-ins with the law. Maybe he'd been hurt or hurt someone else – a car accident, motorcycle wreck, or worse. Malignant disease isn't the first on the list of possibilities for a nineteen-year-old who has never been sick.

"It's a cancerous tumor, Mrs. Richards." Monty later tells me over the phone. "It's eating into the bones in my knee, and that's why I've had so much pain for so long and had to quit my job."

I listen as he proceeds to rattle off the details of his diagnosis and a long list of treatments the doctors are planning with the remarkable aplomb and wordy style that have always been his trademark. He explains osteosarcoma and the medical and surgical interventions he will undergo just like he might expound on any topic of interest – adding a few statistics and a slew of terms he's heard on television or read on the internet.

"They are going to do surgery to scrape out the tumor and graft healthy bone tissue to what's left. After that they'll put some hardware in there to shore up the weak spots in the bone. It's called "limb-sparing" surgery, and it's going to be a long process, but, once I have the operation, I'll be good to go."

Monty always sounds so sure of the truth of what he's saying, which often frustrates his listeners, especially concrete thinkers who aren't buying all his "facts." His amazing aptitude for embellishing mundane details with vivid imagery to boost his credibility very often provokes suspicion in his audience, but not today.

"The bones in my knee and lower leg have been invaded by the tumor, Mrs. Richards, but the cancer hasn't metastasized to other organs, and that's the good news. It only spreads in 1 in 5 cases. The doctors checked out my lungs because that's usually the first place it heads, and I'm clear. I'll have chemotherapy with a mixture of a bunch of different medications to shrink the cancer, and then they'll remove the rest of it in surgery."

"Oh Monty," I say, amazed at his composure in relating all this information. The biopsy was just days ago.

"It's a very rare type of cancer, Mrs. Richards. There are only four hundred cases in the United States every year, and I'm one of them. Lucky me, huh? Even though I'm nineteen, they sent me to a children's hospital because it's a cancer kids get. I bet I've had it for a long time."

He tells me that he thinks the tumor started when he was ten and sprained his knee skiing at the Warner Mountain Ski Hill outside of Lakeview.

"Remember you lent me some skis? I hurt that leg, and it was never right after that. That's when it started, Mrs. Richards. That's when it started. I'm sure of that."

A day after our phone conversation I part the curtains next to Monty's bed in a double room at Seattle Children's Hospital. It's been almost seven years since we've seen each other, and my visit is unannounced. Monty shows no surprise. He greets me just like he always does.

"Hi, Mrs. Richards."

At first glance he's the same old Monty – blonde, freckled, only taller and thinner. He's splayed out on his back, lost in a roiling sea of white linens, but his crimson, grapefruit-sized knee is exposed, propped up on a mound of pillows as a talisman of harsh reality.

A gangly man of around twenty with scraggly dark hair and a five o'clock shadow slouches in a chair at the side of his bed by the windows.

"Jesse, this is Mrs. Richards. She's known me since I was a little kid in Lakeview."

Jesse eyes me impassively. Monty met his friend in a class at Bates Technical College in Tacoma where they were both working to obtain associate degrees in sheet metal fabrication. Monty continues to love animals of all kinds, especially horses, and Jesse's family owns a few. I can see how these two might get along. In contrast to Monty's unusually loquacious and outgoing nature, Jesse is soft spoken and slow to react. Monty's inquisitive, always on the go, and chatters non-stop. Jesse is more laid back – a listener.

Monty asked Jesse to drive him to Seattle a few days ago for his appointment at Children's, and the duo drove to the hospital in Jesse's rusted out junker with holes in the floor and serious mold issues because they had no other transportation. The car barely made it to hospital. Now Monty's been discharged to begin outpatient chemotherapy. He's required to live near the clinics for monitoring and have a caregiver present at all times. Because Monty's Dad, Boone, stepmother Lisa, and Grandma Yvonne work full time at a cafe on the other side of the Tacoma Narrows Bridge nearly two and half hours away and share one working car, staying with Monty in Seattle is out of the question. His sister Christine lives in Lakeview, at least a ten hour drive away. Jesse recently broke up with his girlfriend and is between jobs, so he's agreed to sign on as caregiver even though the two of them have no place to live, no income, and no reliable transportation. As Jesse would later tell me: "We became friends because we liked to play computer games. Monty has something to say about any topic you can think of, and he's always doing something."

Jesse and I maintain our vigil by Monty's bed next to the window for most of the day trying to tune out his roommate's boisterous interactions with his middle school teacher and peers via Skype. A drawn curtain is all that separates us from the loud questions and answers the youngster yells into the computer microphone oblivious to our presence. The boy is pale and bald and looks sick. I realize that Monty's got a different form of the same disease. The thought hurts.

It isn't long before social workers and various medical specialists begin to descend carrying the instructions Monty and Jesse will need for discharge. These teachers are practiced models of efficiency, checking boxes and reciting protocols verbatim from scripts written in language meant to impart the seriousness of Monty's situation and the dire consequences of non-compliance with the rules.

Representatives of various specialties – pharmacy, dietary, chemotherapy clinic, and the like – speed through their printed material with the sing-song intonation and hassled demeanor of flight attendants reeling off rote instructions on seat belt use. They bombard us with a litany of gruesome side effects and draconian changes in every aspect of Monty's life that the treatment of his malignancy will require.

Monty's losses begin to pile up as our clueless instructors press on: "no salad bars, no deli meats, no raw fresh fruit or vegetables" for starters. Eyelashes, hair, hearing, and heart health will be the next to go. As a nurse, I hear the things that remain unsaid. No pardon, no progeny, and no promise of a cure. Monty's limb and possibly his precious life all hang in the balance

"Just another day and another cancer patient," I find my inner troll snarling, as well-meaning medical professionals thumb through page after page of a thick notebook full of instructions, seemingly unaware of the stunned look on our faces. My head feels like a mass of waterlogged batting, my eyes sting, and my throat is tight from suppressing the urge to cry. I'm a middle-aged woman with years of experience working as an RN in hospitals clinics and home health, but the tedious page by page review of this massive life shattering tome is just too much.

Jesse zones, his extremely thin frame folded into a hard plastic chair, gaze fixed on the wall behind the bed as the tutors ramble on. The substance of fear passes between us like an invisible vapor when our eyes meet. Both boys have GED's and no experience with medical lingo or science based therapeutic processes, let alone illnesses like cancer and the horrendous side effects of its treatment. They're out of their league.

My boy's eyes remain closed even as our torturers drone on. I sense he hears every word despite his narcotic stupor, but he remains quiet.

He continues to feign sleep, long after the last medical specialist has left the room.

Monty loves to talk. He always has something to say.

The silence is disconcerting.

## Chapter 6

*"Do not be afraid; our fate cannot be taken from us; it is a gift."*

— Dante Alighieri, Inferno

Sheets of water fall on glass as if poured from a weeping sky as I merge my car onto the freeway on a blustery Thursday evening in February. Jesse and I are racing through the dark toward downtown Seattle to check out temporary housing for cancer patients, while Monty waits for us at the hospital. No rooms are available at the Ronald McDonald House near the hospital, and he's been discharged and needs a temporary place to stay. Jesse and I are searching for room at the inn.

Orbs of jewel-toned light stream from every direction – their filmy glow glimmering off the surface of the Honda's splattered windshield. The windows cloud despite a defroster set on full blast and trusty wipers chop to keep pace with the deluge – their downbeat pumping up the tension. Every lane change is an act of faith, a blind passage through a watery veil with a prayer for mercy. Jesse lowers the passenger side window to peer through the haze for a gap in the steady line of vehicles traveling bumper to bumper kicking up spray. His shaggy hair is damp and matted. His face is wet.

We are an unlikely team, Jesse and I – two strangers from different eras and backgrounds, more different than we are alike, thrown together by chance. Our communications are short and practical. We don't know where we are, or how we got here. We don't know where we're going.

Jesse spies our exit through the mist. The Honda hydroplanes across two lanes to snap into a line of tractor trailers backed up along the ramp toward city central. Muffled honks punctuate the steady roar of cars and semis in our wake as I ease the vehicle behind a string of trucks creeping toward a traffic light and crank a hard right. The massive cancer binder with its reams of paper and multiple tabs thuds to floor as if to remind us of the reason for our quest.

Jesse hunches over, squinting in the light of the open glove compartment to make out the directions to the motel that a nurse scribbled on a paper towel. We zoom down dark alleys between towering brick buildings and circle city blocks lined with cars, straining to find signage in the fog. Jesse finally spots a neon logo and the brightly lit foyer of the cancer hostel on the first floor of a tall building, and we make the rounds again looking for parking. Minutes later I park the Honda a block away, and we race through the downpour toward the entrance.

A somber, round-faced matron waddles over to unlock the door and let us into the lobby where a tall man waits behind a sliding glass panel at the front desk. He pops up to crack it open, and we state our business – our jackets dripping onto the linoleum as he shuffles through our paperwork.

The huge room is furnished with a few pieces of aluminum office furniture gathered around a plastic lawn table heaped with battered magazines. A stack of collapsible wheelchairs rests against the wall in a corner by the door waiting for riders. Sound reverberates off the floor tiles, high ceiling, and huge windows, and there isn't anything soft – no rug or curtains to absorb it. When Jesse and I speak, our voices seem to echo in the large space.

A gaunt boy with white-as-tissue-paper skin and a thin feeding tube taped in his nose rests in an armless chair by the elevators with a dispirited older woman at his side. The two of them stare at us as we approach, but quickly look away. This is no ordinary inn.

It's after eight when Jesse and I finally roll Monty and his meager belongings into the elevator and ascend to the boy's temporary home on the third floor. Monty arrived in Seattle for his appointment with the orthopedic doctor dressed in shorts and a short-sleeved tee-shirt and brought little else. He's wearing my denim jacket and a painful frown as he crutches from his wheelchair and flops onto a queen-size bed by the window. Jesse drags his friend's growing stash of medicines and medical paraphernalia in a borrowed suitcase and dumps its contents on a Formica counter by the television. He peels a banana and offers it to his friend in silence. Monty turns his head.

I sort the enormous bag of colored capsules sent by the pharmacy and plop them into an acrylic pill organizer according to printed instructions attached to each blister pack to make it easier for Jesse, at least for the first month. Jesse is hard to read, but I sense his apprehension. He's been thrust into the uncomfortable role of caregiver with no experience with pharmaceuticals of any kind. We work without talking, unpacking the few groceries we managed to grab, and loading them into a mini-frig.

The large windows of the small motel room are sealed shut and look out on nearby high rise buildings packed along narrow corridors with street lamps haloed in haze. I never expected to be here. I look out at the blurry lights of the Seattle skyline from my place at the foot of Monty's bed considering all that has happened.

I picture Monty as he was on the first day we met – a short, skinny, eight-year-old standing on the front porch. I imagine us walking the pebbled alleys behind my house, tossing seed to the wind, and singing our hearts out. I turn to look at the adult man that boy has become.

The weight of all that's transpired since I traveled from Idaho suddenly hits. The stress of city traffic, the move from hospital to hostel, and our frenetic obsession with the details and logistics of the discharge helped to stave off the horror that's brought us all to this downtown site. Sealed in the silence of his stuffy, sparsely decorated hotel room, harsh reality can't be avoided.

Monty's thin form – still clad in his khaki shorts, tee shirt, and my jacket – lies prone, his angry knee resting on a pillow. Despite his deep voice and blonde facial fuzz, I see him as the child I knew – intelligent, quirky, and immensely wise for his age and background. He's still talkative to a fault, fond of common platitudes, obsessed with animals, snookered by urban legends, and prone to stretching the truth. He still calls me Mrs. Richards.

Thoughts of the future descend like a fleet of giant tractor-trailers bent on overtaking us as they barrel down out of nowhere from deep darkness. Predictable horrors – mouth sores, fevers, nausea, and low blood counts – like crazed demons, lurk along murky side streets ready to t-bone us. There is no other route. Pain is now a passenger. Tears blur our view blinding us to the road ahead. We're navigating unfamiliar territory. And we don't know how we got here. We don't know where we're going.

## Chapter 7

*"Hope" is the thing with feathers*
*That perches in the soul*
*And sings the tune without words*
*And never stops at all"*

— Emily Dickinson

It's an unusually warm spring day when I pull onto a side street in Northeast Seattle after a rainy six-hour trip across Snoqualmie Pass from Idaho. The acrid odor of bus exhaust and the steady drone of combustion engines stopping and going on the wide avenue nearby hit my senses full force when I step out of the car. I'm back in the city. After so many years living in small rural towns, a certain sense of uneasiness descends. I'm not used to all the hustle and hubbub.

I scan both sides of the narrow street to search for the specific building in the Ronald McDonald House (RMH) complex where the two boys have been staying since they left the cancer hotel weeks ago. My first choice proves all wrong, and an attendant directs me to a large facility with an underground parking lot across the way. Bikers speed through on the Burke

Gilman Trail, and children can be seen playing in the grass at Playground Park next door to a tall modern structure with a circular driveway, covered carport, and natural wood beams on a painted facade. The place could pass for a *Shilo Inn,* if it wasn't for the larger than life metal statue of the well-known McDonald's mascot Ronald McDonald sitting cross legged on a bench by the front door.

Affable Ron, in his bright yellow jumpsuit and red and white striped shirt and leggings, welcomes everyone who come to this place, inviting children and even adults to climb on his clown shoes, touch his metallic tuft of flame-like hair, and pat his tummy just as sojourners in centuries past might have reached out to stroke a statue of Mary or one of the Christian saints. Considering Ronald as an icon of transcendence is a bit of a stretch. His wide cherry red grin, bug eyes, and relaxed pose with one leg bent across his knee hardly invoke thoughts of the sacred. But he is friendly looking and familiar. There are people suffering here. It does seem like holy ground.

Security is tight, and I press a button by the front door, introduce myself, and wait until the lock opens to let me in. *Prepare to be humbled,* I tell myself as I step across the threshold. No one wants to think about a child having to face cancer or any serious disease or disability. I silently thank all the McDonald's patrons who toss their change into the collection boxes sitting on checkout counters and drive up windows at over 37,000 McDonalds restaurants worldwide as well as the businesses and churches that contribute to provide for the needs of people who seek this haven. The close monitoring that Monty's treatment requires would not be possible without RMH and the volunteers who provide support.

The space across from the check-in desk is a clone of the waiting areas one sees in so many modern facilities, flush with institutional art, fixtures, and functional furnishings in a boring palette. Mega-couches and chairs arranged in conversational pods seem lost in the massive room with its tall windows, vaulted ceiling, and huge stone fireplace. Commercial grade indoor/outdoor carpeting adds some warmth but hardly makes the place cozy. I scan the room with a critical eye. Better lighting, patterned pillows, and an artificial plant or two might help. The main floor looks like the great room of a budget ski resort without the skis and skiers. It's deserted. A nearby computer lab, video rental office, and outdoor play area are just as empty.

I surrender my driver's license at the check-in desk for vetting, and a clerk calls Monty in his room. I soon spot his lanky form crutching across the lobby to meet me by the front desk. It hurts to see how much weight he's lost since his initial hospitalization. He doesn't smile, but I can tell he's glad to see me and very eager to show me around.

I listen to his spiel about the various services offered at the site as we move around the facility. He imparts this information with authority as if he were an official Ronald McDonald House tour guide. This type of thing is classic Monty, and it makes me smile.

A few families say "hi" as they scurry past us with children in tow. The two of us move on toward a bank of elevators in the back of building. Some people check their mailboxes. Others are heading to resident rooms on the second and third floors or waiting for a lift to the cafeteria downstairs. Monty seems to know everyone.

The dining room is where people gather to cook and eat. A bank of mini-refrigerators lines one wall. Each unit is locked to prevent theft and has been assigned to an individual room to provide space for personal food storage. Clusters of well stocked home economics classroom-style mini-kitchens allow residents to do their own cooking and cleanup.

A Hispanic woman, with a toddler holding onto her skirt, fries tortillas in a cast iron pan on one of the many electric stoves, and the scent of cumin fills the air. A woman in a sari is washing dishes. A man pulling a bald toddler in a red wagon talks on his cell phone in what sounds like Russian while he waits for the elevator. A girl of about four, with blonde fuzz for hair and the standard plastic feeding tube coming out of her nose, sits on her mother's lap reading a book as her little sister plays with toys on the linoleum floor nearby.

Monty's proud to show me the well-stocked food closet in one corner of the dining room filled with staples that are free for the taking: top ramen, various kinds of snacks, and canned goods. He's never known such largesse. He balances his bony frame on his crutches to unlock his fridge for milk to pour on a bowl of corn flakes. He's been on chemo for weeks. His head is hairless and his eyelashes are gone. His face appears gaunt and pasty giving him the look of a wizened albino.

"I don't want to sound like a cry baby, Mrs. Richards," he says, looking down into his bowl, "but chemo gives you such a headache it makes you want to tear your brain out."

We sit in a booth across from the kitchens while he tries to choke down a spoonful of soggy cereal. It's hard to tell if it's fatigue, nausea, the headache, or a combination of all three that's making the act of lifting the utensil to his mouth so difficult. After a few bites he dumps the glop in the trash and calls it good. Monty never had much of an appetite, even as a young child, but this is worrisome.

"They're going to weigh me in tomorrow, Mrs. Richards, and the doctors aren't going to be happy," he says with resignation. "I can't keep anything down."

The medical team ordered one of the ubiquitous feeding tubes to be inserted into Monty's stomach through his nose weeks ago out of concern for his nutritional status and weight loss.

"I had that thing in my nose for less than two hours, and I ripped that sucker out. No way am I going to have that put into me again. No way, Mrs. Richards. They'll have to kill me first."

Cardboard cartons of unopened high calorie liquid nutrition ordered by the medical staff for the detested feedings stand in stacks along one wall in the boy's room as a monument to Medicaid excess. They will eventually go to the landfill.

A pre-teen lad with a swarthy complexion rolls toward us in a wheelchair as we leave the dining area and head for the elevators. Monty stops to chat.

"How's it going, Joey?"

"It's going, Monty," the boy states with the world-weary affect of someone who has traveled the river sorrow. The two boys exchange a few more words and the young lad's downcast spirit is evident. His eyes are averted and he's sighs frequently, but it's the puce tones of his dark complexion and general appearance of ill-health that give me pause. The child's extremely withered lower limb is elevated on the wheelchair's foot rest and looks like a stick of petrified wood with a puny foot and shriveled toes. The sick extremity doesn't look viable.

"That guy's a friend," Monty explains. "He's been under treatment for osteosarcoma for almost a year and had the surgery to remove his tumor, replace his knee, and have a bone graft like I am going to have if all goes as planned."

"My goodness Monty," I say as we're exiting the elevator on third and heading toward his room. "Do you think the doctors are going to be able to save that kid's leg? It doesn't look like it's doing very well."

"That's the hope, Mrs. Richards," Monty says. "That's the hope."

Later we'll see the boy's mother in the elevator on her way up to the cancer unit at the hospital, and she tells us that her son has experienced a setback. The fragile bones in his sick limb snapped while he was transferring from his chair to the bed, and he's in intensive care. My heart goes out to her. It's hard to hear Dickinson's "tune without words" warbled in the dark night of a child's suffering.

But what is the alternative? Submission to medical treatment and all that it entails seems the only choice.

The hoped for cure. That's what we cling to.

## Chapter 8

It's been weeks since my last trip to the Ronald McDonald House, and I've just driven over the pass again for a short visit. The front desk clerk buzzes Monty in his room, and I hear him give the okay for me to head upstairs. He continues the rigorous chemo regime that plagues him with nausea and fatigue. He feel awful most of the time. Communications via Facebook and text, which are Monty's usual vehicles for connecting, have dwindled, but he occasionally calls out of the blue and I've come at his request.

The boys' stuffy motel room at RMH looks like a place where two teenage hoarders have been holed up for months. Mounds of clothing, paperwork, snack wrappers, and the evidence of numerous fast food meals are spread on the heater, floor, and tables, and the place has the distinct odor of squalor. The curtains are drawn and navigating in dark amidst the clutter takes some concentration. No one is surprised when the building inspectors slip a note under the door warning the roommates to clean up empty pizza boxes and open drink containers and other litter. Monty blames Jesse. Things are tense.

"Jesse doesn't even have basic housekeeping skills, Mrs. Richards. He hasn't washed his sheets in months, and they stink...and I mean stink," Monty says with a voice full of righteous indignation.

"And take a look in the bathroom. I'm the only one that cleans it."

He's sitting up in bed and looks even paler and thinner than the last time I saw him. I glance around the room at the piles of trash and clutter and think: *The bathroom is the last place I want to inspect.* I suppress my natural urge to pick up trash and start organizing.

Jesse's slumped against the headboard of his unmade bed like a marionette with limp strings, eyes glued to the computer on his lap. He doesn't respond. Although it's way after two in the afternoon, Monty's "nurse" just rolled out of the sack.

Monty continues to rattle off a litany of gripes after Jesse leaves the room to get breakfast in the cafeteria. With his friend gone he lets loose with all the frustration he's been feeling for months.

"And you know me, Mrs. Richards. I like to have conversations, but Jesse doesn't say anything. I just want someone to talk with...someone who will answer me. When Jesse's not sleeping, he's on his computer. It's like he's not here. He stays up all night playing games and then sleeps the day away like he's in a coma or something. I need communication and companionship."

Two people could not be more different. Monty's known for his way with words and his ability to embellish small amounts of information into a blurry montage of fact and fiction, which can be quite entertaining but also irksome in high doses. Monty likes to argue, but Jesse not so much. They frequently engage in an ongoing feud about the host of the children's television show, *Mr. Rogers Neighborhood*.

"Mr. Rogers was a Navy Seal, Jesse. I've told you that before. He was a sniper with numerous kills to his credit. He wore that sweater to cover the tattoos he got in prison."

"Mr. Rogers was a minister......" Jesse states almost under his breathe.

*Only a Shadow*

"That's what he told people, but he wasn't telling the whole truth of his sordid past," Monty interrupts with utter conviction in his voice. "He was incarcerated for some pretty heinous crimes."

Jesse utters short, passionless denials of Monty's dubious narrative but to no avail.

Monty always sticks to his story.

And Monty has certain passions – Nikola Tesla, *My Little Pony* cartoons, and the makes and models of various car manufacturers. He loves to expound on these topics, if there's someone to listen. Jesse, on the other hand, remains stoic, outwardly calm in every situation, offering very little in the way of feedback. He often communicates in monosyllables, short phrases, or with an understated nod and a stony affect, which makes him hard, if not impossible, to read. On that blustery night in the car, weaving through traffic in downtown Seattle in search of the cancer hostel, Jesse quietly and efficiently put the kibosh on my anxious musings with two words: "Cool it." Amidst the confusion of that mission and even during some of the tensest moments in the hospital, I find Jesse's silent presence, soft deep voice, and simple communication style quite comforting. Not so for Monty. The almost constant nausea and fatigue he feels are making it hard to cope with his friend's habits and overall personality.

"It sounds like you and Jesse needs some space Monty," I offer in Jesse's defense. "You guys are together a lot. This room is awfully small."

But I know there's more going on here than roommate squabbles. Although Monty's friend proudly wears his badge on trips to the hospital, he also seems to be a reluctant caregiver. The medical assistant class that he is required to complete, if he wants to receive money for his services, is paid for in full, but Jesse's moldy car barely runs and the energy required to get himself to the training site in downtown Seattle began to fade on that very first day in the hospital when the nurses were instructing him on how to monitor Monty's temperature.

"I don't care if he needs space, Mrs. Richards," Monty says with anger in his voice. "Jesse's supposed to take care of me. He's supposed to be there when I need help, and he's wasting my money. When I give him cash, he blows it on junk food. I gave him $10, and he came back with a giant bag of caramel corn – a huge bag of complete junk food that I am not supposed to eat."

A sigh escapes before I can stop it. Monty's frequent lengthy discourses on the science of nutrition fail to jive with reality. I listen while he explains his views on the dietary needs of cancer patients.

"Sugar is toxic for me. It feeds the cancer cells. I need wholesome fresh foods to keep my strength up, not the garbage Jesse buys at the Metro with my money."

The boys often shop at the Metropolitan Market next door to RMH. It's an impressive gourmet grocery store and provides one of the few pleasures available to patients like Monty, who suffer with pain, fatigue, and mobility issues and don't have transportation. The aroma of roasted beef and savory sides served by chefs in double-breasted jackets and toques, and the smell of fresh-baked bread and pastries entice shoppers at the door. Fresh- cut flowers, artfully displayed produce, and an amazing selection of imported cheeses and delicacies add to the high-end ambiance of the market, which is a step into the world of the wealthy so different from the Walmart Super Centers and Circle K's that Monty and Jesse are used to.

The finer things in life have their appeal for all of us, but more so for those who rarely have the funds to buy them. People who experience bouts of nausea and face the imperative to keep their weight up, can turn desperate –willing to try just about anything to feel better. The Metro offers tiny seven dollar bottles of artisan water from glaciers in New Zealand, creamy organic smoothies infused with kale and kiwi, and a wide variety of exotic fruit juices at $8.00 or more a pop. These have become more than occasional treats for Monty who purchases them with food stamps.

When Jesse finally returns to the room after breakfast, he's carrying a plastic bag from the market containing Nacho Cheese *Doritos*, a *Mars* bar, and a liter of soda. He sits on his bed and begins to work his way through the snacks. The crunch of corn chips, an occasional slurp of cola, and the click of his computer keys are the only sounds in the room.

Monty is livid. "See what I mean, Mrs. Richards?"

But despite his friend's terse criticism, Jesse soldiers on. He tolerates the seemingly endless rendition of Monty's favorite cartoon episodes with Rainbow Dash, Flutter Shy, and Pinkie Pie's high-pitched voices playing night and day. Jesse endures Monty's frequent bouts of anger, caustic jibes about his care giving, habits, and personality. He has the strength of character to take the tension of communal living with normal life on hold, and he sticks it out. I think he sees something in Monty he admires but is unable to put into words.

Family visits are few and far between, but Monty's brother Daniel sometimes stops by for a short stay after work. His clothes are grimy, and he looks tired and gaunt, his face drawn into a permanent frown. He works long and hard hours at a salvage yard. Daniel blames the doctors for his brother's plight, claiming that they reportedly blew off Monty's requests for an MRI.

"They told Monty that there were other people who needed an MRI more than he did. It was because he didn't have insurance. They let him go and now *this*." Daniel pumps the air with his fist. Monty's brother looks so thin – almost cachectic. He is such a handsome man, and it's hard to see him so wasted. His anger seems to be eating him up.

"How about dinner and a movie tonight," I suggest in an attempt to lift the somber mood that hangs over the three of us as we sit talking after Daniel leaves. This type of outing has become routine on my trips west, because I have transportation and the funds to help Monty and Jesse do some of the things they would normally enjoy. Volunteers at RMH work hard to provide entertainment – bus trips to the mall, movies, communal meals and the like – but finding relief from the daily grind of the cancer experience takes so much energy – energy that's needed just to cope.

"The days all blend together," Jesse offers during one of the rare times he's moved to share about his experience of living at RMH.

"You're thrown together with people you would never normally hang with. Some of them don't even speak your language. No one here is really living, They're just going through the motions on autopilot. After three weeks in this place people are completely changed. You won't recognize them. It's the stress."

On this particular evening the three of us head out to El Rancho for an evening's reprieve. The restaurant is crowded, and we slide into a booth in back by the bathrooms. Canned mariachi music blasts through speakers on the wall and place smells of the rancid oil in which the "homemade" tortillas chips are most certainly frying. Dusty artificial flowers on every sticky table do little to improve the ambiance.

When our food finally comes, Monty is too sick to talk much or even take a bite of his burrito. Jesse and I chew in silence, eating as if it were an onerous job that we needed to finish before Monty tosses his cookies watching us. We can't get going fast enough.

Once inside the movie theatre, Monty orders two over-sized boxes of Skittles and a giant soft drink at the concession counter. His long lecture on cancer nutrition earlier in the day is still fresh in our minds but Jesse and I don't comment.

The sound track for *Iron Man III* thunders as we stare up at the screen from the front row. Jesse points out that Monty has been warned to avoid loud noises because of hearing damage from the chemo, and he looks at Monty as if expecting a response.

"Is that true Monty?" I ask, knowing that it's not going to make a difference. We're here to watch the movie...to escape.

Jesse shrugs and looks back at the screen.

Monty stares ahead, chomping on his candy and slurping his Sprite. He just won't accept another loss. Not tonight

## Chapter 9

*"Fear is a universal experience.
Even the smallest insect feels it."*

— Pema Chodron
When Things Fall Apart:
Heart Advice for Difficult Times

It's May when I feel the impulse to return to Seattle. As fate would have it, I am in the right place at the right time. Monty has a tedious roster of diagnostic tests scheduled to check if the chemo is working, and the medical team plans to meet with him once the reports from all the scans and examinations come in. By some kind of miracle, the three of us will be together when Monty talks to his doctor. I am not an official badge-wearing caregiver at his point, nor have I ever been asked to sign any type of release of information form. No one questions my presence during medical consultations and exams, and any and all medical information is freely disclosed to me. I imagine that some people at this pediatric facility assume that I am Monty's mother.

I leave my brother and sister in-law's house in Enumclaw at 5 a.m. to make it to the hospital in time for the first appointment.

Vehicles are already inching along I-5 seventeen miles outside of downtown Seattle at this early hour. I weave the Honda in and out of traffic in narrow lanes packed with semis and vans, taking a sip of my Venti Americano every time the traffic rolls to a complete stop. I'm never certain if I'll get anywhere on time in this city. There's a drawbridge on the route to the hospital that threatens to stop traffic for forty-five minutes or more. A highway reader-board warns travelers of its imminent lifting, and there was a time visiting Monty when I beat the clock with only minutes to spare. As if I am not already frazzled.

I arrive at the door of the boy's room at 7:45 a.m., and the three of us head out for the first appointment. Jesse pushes Monty's wheelchair on the path behind the private apartments and various buildings that comprise the RMH campus, and I walk beside them. The spring air is cool and infused with a whiff of lilac. We hear birds tweeting in the trees. Buses and cars whiz by as we wait for the light on the main street in front of hospital and wind our way up the hill to the entrance to the clinics on the seventh floor.

Of course I've been to Seattle Children's with Monty before but navigating the complicated floor plan of this mammoth facility does not come easily. It's a giant labyrinth of nature wings: Ocean, River, Forest, Frog, Mountain, Whale, each with its own puzzling elevator system, bright signage, and snaking hallways covered with ribbons of color and murals on a theme. Something about the layout is disorienting. Am I floundering in River or set adrift in Ocean? Which elevator should I take – Frog...Whale...Bear? The corridors are a maze of seemingly endless, often windowless tubes, many cordoned off with metal doors that lead to restricted areas that can leave a person feeling simultaneously locked in and locked out – lost in space, trapped in a medical matrix with no clear sense of location in reference to the rest of the world or how to find an exit.

Even with a color-coded map in hand, I sometimes make a wrong turn, take an elevator to nowhere, or arrive on a strange floor without a clue of where I am. The solution comes when my longstanding coffee habit forces me to memorize the way to three different Starbucks kiosks on different floors. Sugary caffeinated drinks replace most meals when I'm at the hospital for any length of time.

Jesse and I roll Monty to clinic intake area. This is one spot that's easy to find. Monty carries a long strip of bar-coded labels that he's asked to surrender at each entry point so that the staff can determine his precise location at any time as he moves through the medical machine.

Every receptionist in the building greets Monty with "Date of birth?" in lieu of a more standard greeting before beginning a finger dance on the keyboard. Monty looks pained when asked to repeat his birthday for the umpteenth time. He croaks one word answers to polite inquiries about how he is doing. He's usually so upbeat, but today he seems morose, slumping in his chair like a deflated version of his former self.

Check-in clerks scan us to determine who we are, where we've been, and where we are headed, even if we're not sure. MRI, CT scan, PET scan, echocardiogram, and hearing assessment – Jesse and I check off tests one by one. Seattle Children's system runs with a sensitive efficiency which is truly amazing. The staff graciously attempts to ease the trauma of our packed schedule by insuring that Monty's movement through the system is as smooth as possible. The PET scan lab techs allow a short rest in a dark room because Monty complains of nausea. His purple VIP pass bumps him up to the front of every line. Jesse and I are so busy time seems to melt away.

I'm surprised when an attendant asks if I would like to stay in the room during the MRI.

"It's a children's hospital, Mrs. Richards," Monty says with disgust. "These people are used to having parents stay in the room with their kids."

His perception that he is being treated like a little child only adds to his sense of powerlessness.

"But you can stay, Mrs. Richards. I can use the company."

An attendant hands me ear plugs and a stack of *People* magazines and offers me a seat in the corner, while he slides Monty off the gurney, straps him feet first onto a sliding table, and inserts him into what looks like a large plastic donut covered with glossy animal stickers. A small mirror attached to Monty's head allows him to watch a Disney movie playing on a big screen on the far wall, while he remains perfectly still on his back. Our eyes meet in the mirror, and he offers a thumbs-up.

I hear the radiology technicians talking, chuckling, and see them gesturing to each other through a heavy glass window next to my chair. Their guffaws can be heard over the deafening whirl of the MRI machine despite my heavy-duty earplugs.

The capricious, inequitable, isolating nature of illness stings.

*How can these people be so callous? Don't they see that someone is hurting here? These strong, healthy men yuck it up, untouched by the trouble that this young man is living.*

I try to remind myself that every life includes pain. Who knows what these men are facing or will face in the future? I'm sure that in all the years I worked as a nurse that I too had my moments of raucous laughter with my co-workers in earshot of patients' dealing with the anxiety and heartache of serious illness. As Pope Francis says: "Who am I to judge?" Yet my anger resurfaces. It seems just plain *wrong* to laugh in this place.

After the MRI, Monty passes his hearing test with only a slight change detected. With that bit of good news we're done. It's 4 p.m., and, through the miracle of communication technology, every piece of the medical puzzle has already snapped into place. A team of medical professionals has assembled at the orthopedic clinic to deliver their report.

Monty, Jesse, and I sit shoulder to shoulder on plastic chairs in the corner of a walk-in closet-sized space facing a social worker, oncology nurse, and doctor. Monty's scan results glow on an open laptop sitting on a counter across from an examination table pushed against the wall. The room is too small for six people.

Dr. Conrad leans against the exam table facing us, his long legs and arms crossed as if bracing for a fight. He's a middle-aged man who's treated numerous cases of osteosarcoma. He's dedicated his life to fighting this awful scourge despite the limited number of drugs and treatments in his arsenal.

It's the nurse practitioner assigned to Monty's care who delivers the results of the tests. She's dealt with Monty's quirky personality for months and been in charge of monitoring his blood work and nagging him about his weight and issues of non-compliance. Her initial statement is blunt and to the point, and the information she imparts is soon confirmed by Dr. Conrad.

No matter who tells us or what words they use, the truth remains the same. The tumor has grown despite the torturous treatments that have brought its host to his knees. There's suspicious spot on one lung. The affected limb will have to go.

As a nurse I'm practiced in helping patients under my care accept their losses, pick up the pieces, and work with what's left, but I find myself less objective here. My fragile hold on hope begins to crumble. The words of the medical team sink in, bending me to the floor, cutting my resolve off at the knees, amputating a piece of me. Monty cries out briefly. He immediately expresses concern for his brother, and how he will take the news. Jesse's face is a blank slate, but I sense his shock.

A specialist enters the room to measure Monty for prosthesis before anyone can protest. The man is all business, unintentionally force feeding us a hefty serving of reality regardless of hard it is to swallow. He carries a flesh colored wooden leg with an unrealistic looking foot, its toenails painted red. Monty, Jesse, and I stare down at the crude device as he holds it up to Monty's sick extremity for measurement. "Too soon!" cries my inner troll. "Too soon!" But I don't want to make a scene.

Monty's resilient nature is on full display as he grills the prosthetics technician on various options he's read about trolling the internet. He rambles on about carbon fiber sockets, spring foot plates, and the C-leg, using technical jargon that makes him sound on top of the topic and technology.

"I'm going to opt for the C-leg," he announces with confidence. "It has a microprocessor with sensors in the knee and ankle."

The prosthetics specialist listens while Monty expounds on the benefits of the C-leg. The technician doesn't let on that C-legs are state-of-the-art artificial legs for above the knee amputees that are neither attainable nor suitable for most people. He doesn't let on that C-legs cost as much as $70,000 or point out that Monty is a Medicaid patient, which pretty much insures that his new limb will be the cheapest low-tech model available.

No one broaches the topic of prognosis. But the words of the nurse practitioner play over and over on an invisible tape in my mind. "There is a suspicious spot on one lung....a suspicious spot.....a suspicious spot."

Medical treatment is failing.

The fury I feel toward the prosthesis expert's hasty intrusion is replaced with overpowering fear. Why is this happening to this beautiful boy?

And out of nowhere comes the question. Where is God? How can a loving God let this happen?

I am afraid Monty is going to die.

## Chapter 10

> "The border says stop to the wind, but the
> wind speaks another language, and keeps
> going."
>
> — Alberto Rios
> The Border: A Double Sonnet

In 1963, on a rocky cliff overlooking the Atlantic Ocean, a young girl sits basking in sunlight, reveling in her solitude. She's spending a week at Blue Bay Girl Scout Camp on Long Island in East Hampton and has wandered away from her campsite for an unauthorized break to explore the headlands overlooking the sea. She's a skinny thirteen-year-old wearing cut-offs over a one-piece bathing suit, flip flops, and a triangular madras scarf tied in her sun-bleached hair. Her bronzed skin glows with summer, cooled by an offshore breeze after the climb up the rocky ledge.

An endless ocean blurs on the horizon, and she closes her eyes to take in the seaweed smells and taste the salty mist. Gulls swoop and glide. A jetty reaches its arm into the vast waters to accept the relentless waves that pummel and caress *it with foamy glee. Wisps of white cross the azure heavens, as if compelled by an unseen magnet. This panorama, unsullied by the flotsam and jetsam of human activity and development, stretches the girl's thoughts toward mystery, like sirens calling from the sea. It will be many decades before she finds words for this moment, but there is a sense that something is moving in her as well...something momentous.*

Every camper attending Blue Bay Girl Scout Camp in the summer of 1963 was severely warned to stay away from those rocky bluffs, which naturally led to an unholy fascination with them. One steep precipice by the fire pit where scouts gathered for marshmallow roasts and sing-alongs most evenings was cordoned off with chicken wire. This was the reported site where one hapless camper veered too close to the edge and tumbled over rocks through heavy brush to the beach below. The story of the young teen's catastrophic injuries, a campfire legend, circulated through the ranks of newbies on the salty ocean breeze.

I couldn't stop thinking about the unfortunate girl's broken body splayed in the brambles at the cliff's sandy base. Alone in my sleeping bag at night, I dreamed about her fall and ruminated on rumors that she spent years bedridden in a total body cast under her mother's care – a teenage nightmare to be sure. Details of the tragic accident, inked into young psyches, drew many girls to venture over to the flimsy barrier to see just how steep the drop was. One day I got the urge to check the cliff out for myself.

At this stage of life it's hard to get in touch with the adolescent hubris that led me to leave my unit on that summer afternoon to spend an hour scrambling over scraggly vegetation and scree to scale that precipice. Perhaps it was a combination of the seductive nature of the forbidden, the exhilaration of my free agent status away from parental scrutiny, along with the lack of oversight by our teenage counselors, many of whom were only a year or two older than their charges. Maybe I can blame an overactive imagination or hormones that sparked a rare episode of adolescent defiance. I was a clueless thirteen-year-old growing up in the 60s, and the stereotypical teenage rebellion wasn't yet on my radar. I listened to the Beach Boys and Herman's Hermits, and sang Johnny Angel in the shower. I spent most summers lounging at the town pool with my girlfriends, riding my bike around the neighborhood, or looking forward to Friday night pajama parties. I pledged allegiance to one nation under God, attended weekly Girl Scout meetings and Sunday school, and sang *Kumbayah* by the campfire with my peers. I never got in trouble for anything more serious than loafing on the job as a candy striper or whispering and passing notes in study hall to my best friend, Alice. I colored inside the lines.

Looking back from the comfort of my granny rocker half a century later, I see that venturing off alone to climb a cliff may have been sparked by that young girls fall and my fascination with the notion of mortality. My Grandpa Ernest, who was a part of my daily life, had died from a heart attack the year before while weeding his garden. His death was sudden and final and evoked a number of questions.

I was generally a compliant teen, only occasionally balking at my parents edicts. When expected to spend boring Saturdays at Uncle Ernie's duplex in Levittown or accompany the family on what seemed like an endless succession of outings to the 1964 World's Fair, I often resorted to putting my protests in writing. These treatises, written in quasi-legal terminology on a sheet of plain notebook paper, were designed to convince my father to consent to an alternative activity for the weekend. It was a novel approach that appealed to Dad's soft heart and love of logic. These literary masterpieces often changed his mind. All children should feel so empowered.

Perhaps early success with written arguments fed a budding independent streak that enabled me, as naïve as I was, to feel comfortable pushing limits. Perhaps it fueled the gumption it took to break the rules. It may have also led to some other trouble at camp.

Running along one of the sandy trails between campsites one morning with a few of my tent mates, a senior counselor summoned me out of the group and told me to follow. I soon found myself marching toward a Jeep parked in the middle of a dirt road. Three middle-aged, outdoorsy looking women dressed in khaki shorts and matching camp shirts exited the vehicle with remarkable efficiency of motion as if conducting a military maneuver and stood at attention in formation behind the running vehicle. The tallest of the three, a stone-faced matron with weathered skin, was wearing a canvas boonie hat with a long drawstring and combat boots. She stood arms crossed, wide-stance while her cohorts looked on.

I had been sending numerous postcards inscribed with romantic messages in rhyming verse on the order of "roses are red" from a fictional character named Woy-Toy through the camp post office. I'd spent considerable time crafting these silly poems, addressing them to the kids in my tent to the amusement of myself and my fellow campers. The matron towered over my small quaking frame, calling me to task for clogging the inter-camp mail and requesting that I cease and desist. How they identified me as Woy Toy remains a mystery. It took a while for my legs to stop shaking after they left. I was not used to getting in trouble with the law and this was not good. The man upstairs was watching. This was the only kind of God I knew – the one ready to squash the insolent for any and all infractions.

Almost every one of my peers went to a church of some kind when I was growing up, and the existence of God was a given. When a classmate named Barbara declared her atheism in the locker room after seventh grade gym class one day, everyone stared at her, speechless. As inculcated into the 1960s culture of Christianity as we were, atheism wasn't an option we considered. Even though my parents were "Chreaster Christians," who rarely darkened the doorway of a church except for Christmas Eve and Easter, they did insist that I have a firm foundation in the tenets of the Lutheran faith and dutifully sent me for two years of religious instruction. But there was nothing about my experience of catechism class to lift my thoughts beyond myself. The religion I saw there smacked of the "step on a crack and you'll break your mother's back" kind of superstition. Prayers were like letters to Santa. God loomed as a vengeful punisher and "you better watch out, you better not cry, you better not pout." The thought occurs to me that a trip to *Santa's Workshop* in the Catskills might have been the very beginning of my long slow slide to agnosticism. Perhaps there is where my doubts began.

A black and white photo of my mother, sister, and me posing by a frozen pole documents our family's visit to this destination resort in 1957. A sullen looking elf, perched on top of a six-foot cylinder of ice holds a sign that informs visitors that they have arrived at the actual "North Pole," the legendary facility where Santa Claus lives and works and has his being. The column's icy crystals glistened like magic in the blazing summer sun which only added to the mystical aura of the place.

"How does the pole stay frozen in this hot weather?" I asked my engineer Dad as I scratched the cold surface of the crystalline cylinder with the inquisitive fingers of a seven year old.

"How can reindeer fly? How does Santa get all the bikes and big stuff in the sled?" I inquired, staring at the classic sleigh decorated with jingle bells and ropes of tinsel and eyeing Donner and Blitzen munching mounds of hay in Kris Kringle's barn.

"Santa has his magic ways," I imagine my daddy answering with a slight smile, which I failed to detect because of my absolute trust in parental wisdom.

"He knows whether you've been naughty or nice."

Our little family was leaving Schraft's Restaurant on Jericho Turnpike heading to our car on a frosty Christmas Eve the following winter, when I thought I spotted a reindeer-drawn sleigh outlined in colored lights snaking across the night sky. I was sure I heard the tinkle of sleigh bells, the crack of a whip, and Rudolph's whinny as the merry old man and his team streaked into the starry heavens. Any doubts that might have surfaced were swept away by the awe of the imaginary vision and my faith in Santa was further vindicated the next morning when I found a cherry red Schwinn with a basket and fat tires under the tree, just as I'd hoped.

But it's no surprise that skepticism about Santa continued to surface. Earnest questions about reindeer flying and the shear logistics of making worldwide deliveries in a single night found a voice. Rumors were circulating at school. Too many tales of giant rabbits hopping during the night filling baskets with cellophane grass, jelly beans, and colored eggs fueled my doubts. An obese man in red fur sliding down chimneys didn't jive with my newly acquired understanding of the ways of the world.

Today my mother's enigmatic smile jumps out at me from that old black and white photo by the pole. She's sporting the same bemused look she wore on the day we stood by the refrigerator in our kitchen in Floral Park, and I finally got the nerve to ask the question point blank. Just as Charles Webb's mother did in his poem *The Death of Santa Clause*: "Tears in her throat, the terrible news rising in her eyes," my mother took my hand.

Half a century later I still remember the power of that instant, the sinking feeling of emptiness as the promise of the good and goods that Santa embodied vaporized. That pole in the Catskills was a phony monument to refrigeration technology – the whole Santa saga, a silly ruse, a fiction fabricated for gullible children to make them toe the line, and I'd fallen for it. In that instant, a sliver of childish understanding vanished and a certain cynicism took its place. Later it would be apparent that the loss of Santa was the first step, a rite of passage, in the movement from childish idealism and an innocent black and white view of the world toward maturity. The leap from the loss of Santa to the loss of God would take years. Over time all truth would come in shades of gray.

The bold strokes necessary to buck the waves of the zeitgeist of the 60s and 70s were not for me, and I spent precious years treading water in the murky morass of religious limbo. I gave nary a thought to the effects of my wandering ways or where they might be leading, choosing the itinerary of my life without serious reflection or even a nod to anything bigger and more important than myself. Like most of my species, I was itching for something new and drawn to the forbidden. I became intoxicated with the exhilarating power to choose. And I was not alone. Just about the time I gave up composing romantic rhymes in iambic pentameter, Girl Scout meetings, and long summer days with nothing to do but recline on a towel by the pool, I gave up God.

Breaking free of the stuffy naughty or nice religion of my youth came easy. The times were changing as they always do. No need to pen long documents in legal jargon to argue my case, I was my own master. Like many of my generation, I set about forging my own crooked path, ignoring rules, falling into step with the trends of times, blunting the edges of right and wrong, and employing the mantra "to each his own" as a cover for my many desires. I was a kid in a candy shop, and I sampled my share of its wares.

But the conundrum of the ever-present, inequitable nature of suffering caught my attention. After college I worked as a nurse in a county hospital. Every day brought more examples of the horrible adversities befalling ordinary people: a four year old child dying from a brain tumor; a twenty-two year old with terminal melanoma; a baby in a coma after falling into a backyard swimming pool. A single experience at the bedside of a paralyzed girl in 1973 troubled me for decades. Why was I thoughtlessly moving through my life worried about frivolous details like where to go out to eat, what to wear, and what movie to watch, when my patient would never walk or use her hands again? How could a loving God allow such abject suffering?

Sometimes I wish for the power to erase the memories and

missteps that came with that period of spiritual limbo in my late teens and early twenties. Pain became my teacher as I struck out on a meandering course, rejecting the religion of my childhood and its threats of perdition to search for my own brand of "spirituality." Like so many privileged Boomers, I was swept away by the current of the culture and followed my bliss on the wings of pride and skepticism. Some decisions from that era continue to break my heart.

But that mysterious calling from that rocky cliff overlooking the ocean so long ago would not let me go. On that day in Seattle, standing in the exam room with my beautiful boy and my fear, I reached out to the "unknown God," and I felt him near. After years dabbling in numerous Protestant varieties of Christianity, inwardly struggling with the problem of pain, God opened another door for me and I walked through it. What a strange, convoluted journey it has been since that moment in the sun.

## Chapter 11

Monty and I are up at the crack of dawn on the morning after the disastrous clinic meeting. Bright sunshine glints off the glass and steel facade of the brand new cancer wing as we amble toward the hospital to check into the oncology ward and hop back on the treatment treadmill. Surgery might not mean a total cure. The chemo must continue. The very idea of amputation seems unreal, a vague dream, a hideous nightmare that will never happen. We're awake now. It's back to business as usual.

Monty's excited to show me the "the Penthouse" – the brand-new wing of the children's hospital that contains a state of the art center for youngsters with cancer that recently opened. We both marvel at modern engineering as the elevator ceiling lights sparkle in green and blue on our assent to the eighth floor.

The windows by the entrance to the oncology unit look out on a large flat roof covered with what looks like dirty cheese cloth. Scruffy, unidentifiable plants...possibly weeds...poke up from the webbing like the sparse hairs of the nearly bald heads so common in this place.

"That's going to be a rooftop park," Monty tells me with his classic brand of optimism, "so the patients can go outside."

I stare at the bleak expanse from the giant windows,

wondering if this is true. The scene evokes textbook images of the aftermath of an atomic bomb. This is the last dismal view of the outside world that Monty and other cancer patients will see before entering the isolation of the cloistered chemotherapy unit, sometimes for long periods of time. I try to envision greenery flourishing on the roof – children playing or wheeling themselves around in their wheelchairs – but it doesn't compute. The large steel doors to the cancer unit crack apart, and we scuttle through the opening before they snap shut like a giant clam.

Chrome modules with heavy glass fronts line both sides of the hallway like massive blocks of ice in metal frames stacked end to end, each a temporary treatment cell for a youngster with cancer. One imagines the children in these cubicles incubating in pods like a scene from an old sci-fi flick, each one sealed with a spring-loaded sliding glass door. Even the bathroom is a cube of clear glass surrounded by nylon curtains on a track. The decor inside is functional and futuristic: chairs and hassocks on wheels done in psychedelic orange and lime that can be moved around to rearrange the space and a cushioned cubicle built into the far wall that often serves as a bed for overnight visitors. Everything feels new and modern. Only the standard motorized bed with its bleached linens and stainless steel side rails and "Welcome Monty" scrawled on a low-tech white board seem familiar.

Monty's regular room on the oncology floor seems perpetually dark. One window to the outside overlooks a narrow architectural cylinder packed with vegetation – another disheartening scene that only enhances the room's claustrophobic feel. A big screen television attached to the wall plays a video to impart information about the hospital's rules and programs and welcome the newcomers. Monty clicks it off.

"Been there, done that." he says jumping into bed.

He climbs between the sheets to begin surfing on his hospital issue laptop waiting for staff to descend and begin the usual routine. Snarls of electric cords and ominous looking machinery form a web around the bed. An aide enters with a pitcher of ice water warning him to stay hydrated. Monty snarls like a surly teenager.

"I know, I know," he says, waving the aide away with the back of his hand. He spits out his words through gritted teeth.

The admission proceeds with efficient precision which is the way all things are done at Seattle Children's. Bags of IV fluid and tubing on a pole standing guard at the door ready to serve. Various staff members rush in and out to complete their assigned missions. Within minutes a dark fluid, the color of butterscotch, flows from a plastic bag into a port in Monty's chest. Despite the dismal report we heard yesterday, we pray that something will change and the chemo's toxins will find their target. It's the only way to stay sane.

Out of nowhere the sliding glass door opens and a "patient navigator" enters the room. Many loving souls with tender spirits have knocked on the chrome molding of Monty's cell – chaplains, patient writing project coordinators, and purveyors of various Children's Hospital programs aimed at improving the quality of young patient's lives. They are nice people with sincere intentions and valuable programs, but there seems no way to stop their intrusions. Perhaps because it is a pediatric hospital, tacit approval of these staffer's entrance into the room is a given.

"I can't take any more of these people bopping in and out of here, Mrs. Richards," Monty grumbles one day. "I don't have the energy for new relationships."

I've noticed that even rare visits from friends and acquaintances from Monty's past can take a toll. The mother of a friend from high school arrives to deliver her manifesto on the power of prayer, which she dispatches using classic Christian speak. I know she means well, but she stays too long – pressing for the gory details, talking too much, not listening, draining our reserves from the effort it takes to be polite. When she's gone, it is such a relief.

"I don't mind hearing that people are praying for me, Mrs. Richards," Monty confided after the woman left. "I need all the help I can get, but I can do without all that talk."

"She is trying to show she cares Monty, but it can get old when the person speaking has no idea what it's like to live in your skin, and it seems like she is just passing through to deliver their religious script. There may be love behind what she says and all her inquiries, but sometimes it doesn't feel like it."

But not all visitors are a burden. It's at least a ten hour drive for Monty's sister, Christine, to get to Seattle from Lakeview, and she makes the trip several times to show her love. Monty positively glows when his niece climbs on his bed to show him her toys. Chris and her daughter Ophelia are better medicine than any doctor can provide. Even his stepdad, Rick, makes the trip.

When we're alone in the room we don't talk about yesterday's report. The professional staff members who provide Monty's care certainly know about his impending surgery, but surprisingly only one young nurse mentions the amputation.

"Some bad news yesterday, huh," she comments, her eyes focused on the IV machine, which she adjusts with both hands while she speaks.

"Yeah" Monty says, without further comment.

The nurses and doctors with their rolling technology disappear behind tasks and protocol and most don't seem to see the need for anything more. I understand. I was once just like them over forty years ago, a young RN with too much to do and not enough time to do it, buzzing from one hospital room to the next, never stopping to acknowledge a patient's concerns beyond any physical needs that could be addressed. Medical tasks were a shield and armor against getting too close and draconian job expectations made it easy to overlook the emotional needs of the people under my care. I didn't have time.

Modern medical environments, especially cancer units, can be isolating. Any and all contact with other patients and their visitors is cut off out of concern for the compromised immune systems of the children under treatment. This prison-like atmosphere, along with the constant drive for data and documentation, makes it even easier for staff to avoid addressing a patient's sorrow and all the other emotions that arise in cancer's wake. The halls are lined with medical professionals perched on stools typing away and others pushing their devices on wheels. Computers eat up time at the expense of human touch and interaction in the service of so-called quality assurance. The result for those like Monty, who submit to their treatments without the daily help of family because they have no other recourse, is a long loneliness.

Amidst these sad thoughts a tiny woman with a pixie haircut enters the room carrying a guitar. She's a petite twenty-something with wide smile and sweet persona. She offers her heart and her art, encouraging Monty to write the lyrics to his own song.

I hear the therapist strum her guitar and put his words to music. Her voice is lilting, and the tune is simple.

*Friends and friends coming in together*
*Coming in, looking out for each other's back*
*United we are facing*
*The cruel world we are invading.*

Monty and I are blessed by this woman's presence, and yet there is no doubt that this truly seems a cruel, cruel world.

Later Monty posts on Facebook:

*Well I guess it's about time I inform everyone on the latest news from all the tests I got. There was no improvement in the tumor in the bone of my leg, it actually got worse so...big news is my leg is getting amputated just above the knee. I am not sad or upset about it, as I say if something is broken and can't be fixed might as well replace it. My surgery is next week on the 15th. I will be waking up with a prosthetic leg so hope it all goes well. All I ask is in any reply to this please don't ask if I am sad or hurt about it. I am fine with the decision, and what's done is done. My new nickname is the "One Leg Wonder."*

## Chapter 72

Jesse, Monty, and I don't have much to say on the morning of the surgery. No one moves to turn on the light when the alarm sounds at 8 a.m. in the boy's dank, airless room at RMH. The curtains are drawn, and the digital face of the clock provides the only light.

Monty groans and turns over, and I stretch on a cot crammed against the wall across from his bed trying to rouse from deep sleep. Monty was awake most of the night guzzling apple juice from a gallon bottle trying to stave off the awful nausea that plagues him. He was instructed to take nothing by mouth after 4 a.m. The half-filled cider jug rests on its side amidst a mass of tangled bedding along with his computer remote, crumpled pre-op instructions, and the other detritus of restless sleep. The place smells like a locker room, and the clutter and garbage that the boys have accumulated over months of household neglect only add to the oppressive sense of gloom and doom permeating the space.

Jesse and I both get up and dress and then plop down on the roll-away bed to hold watch, while Monty gathers his papers to get ready to go to the hospital. He's dressed in the same shorts and T-shirt he slept in. We sit in silence as our boy swings his legs over the side of his bed and starts to ceremoniously inscribe an epitaph on his left thigh with a black Sharpie:

"Property of Monty McDonald June 27, 1993-May 15, 2013, R.I.P."

Monty draws a dotted line around the circumference of his leg about six inches above his knee, and then a row of tiny scissors each a precise replica of the one before it. He takes his time.

Jesse and I wait at the foot of this horrifying cross as our friend prepares.

"The trip to the hospital will be my last walk on two legs, and I'm saying goodbye," Monty tells us without looking up.

Jesse and I say nothing. We listen as Monty recants how he's argued with the medical staff about being able to keep his amputated limb.

"I want them to give it to me," he says, patting his lower leg with affection.

"What would you do with it Monty?" I ask, suspecting that a hypo-crisis like this helps him to focus on a small grievance to avoid feeling overwhelmed.

"It's mine. I was born with it, and it's been part of me since June 27, 1993. I own it, and they won't let me keep it."

"I'm sure there are rules about that sort of thing, Mont."

"Stupid rules. Stupid laws. Stupid Cancer."

"Stupid Cancer," the three of us repeat in unison.

Jesse, Monty, and I all wear green wristbands stamped with the words *Stupid Cancer* in bold letters. Monty's family purchased them at the hospital gift shop. The phrase was coined by a twenty-one-year-old college student diagnosed with pediatric brain cancer in 1995, who later founded a non-profit advocacy organization for young adults suffering from the disease. *"Stupid Cancer"* has become our mantra.

Once outside the RMH, we consciously slow our pace along the familiar paved path behind the buildings of the campus.

We pass a concrete slab ringed with a few wooden seats

where Monty, Jesse, and I gathered the day before with a motley crew of RMH residents and their families during a fire drill. The alarm sounded around two in the afternoon and everyone fled to the patio. There we stood together, a patchwork of human diversity, disability, and disease – a sweaty human family of sick children and their weary caregivers, united in adversity, waiting for the fireman's all clear, lingering on borrowed time.

I love that humble square of cement with its benches, as much as I love the strip of pavement meandering through a wooded glade toward the hospital. They both offer a place to touch nature in the center of a noisy urban setting. It is nature that "never did betray." It is nature that reassures us "all that we behold is full of blessing." (Wordsworth) I imagine that legions of people have paused to take a breather on these seats to study the sky and ponder the beauty of the surrounding trees and foliage and to smell the flowers along this undulating path.

All three of us notice the spindly aspens with brass plaques, benches inscribed with names and dates, as well as the poems and epitaphs on stakes tucked into flower beds and bushes – all memorials for children lost. The trip toward the hospital intake and pre-op holding area is Monty's version of the Via Dolorosa, but there is no cheering or jeering crowd – only the spirits of young souls who have gone before. They remind us to treasure each moment, and we do.

Too soon we arrive at the pre-op check-in. An anesthetist meets with us to assure Monty that an epidural will eliminate his immediate post-op pain. This is the site where Monty is questioned, stripped, and eventually led down a long hall toward a modern operating room to his own version of Golgotha.

Jesse and I watch as he crutches down a long hallway and slips through yet another set of steel doors.

Monty does not look back.

## Chapter 13

*"Our lives are in Your hands....."*

A phrase from the refrain of
***Only a Shadow***
By Carey Landry

A nurse ushers Jesse and me out of the pre-op exam room into an open area where the families of beloved children undergoing surgery sit to wait and worry. A clerk at a central desk offers us a pager like those distributed in restaurants to signal when a table is ready. Our only task for hours to come will be holding this weighty device close to check and re-check it for a blinking light that will indicate that someone is available to give us a report on how Monty's surgery is progressing.

The assembly of waiters, of which Jesse and I are now a part, slouch in rows of chairs arranged face to face. Few people are talking. Relatives and friends gather in pods, staring at screens, tapping and swiping, or sitting like catatonics captivated by an alternative reality that no one else can see.

Small children wiggle and fuss as parents struggle to keep them entertained. Every once in a while a toddler lets out a shrill howl of shear frustration as if to siphon off some of the anxiety that's percolating in the room. Women in burkas and rainbow colored headscarves, lumberjacks in plaid wool and dirty Levis, and yuppies in polyester Dockers and polo shirts have all found themselves in this strip of a room. Although we don't communicate aloud, we are sisters and brothers, each praying in our own way for good news about a child we love.

Intermittent calls for patients and medical staff blast over the public address system, and an occasional loud phone conversation in a foreign tongue breaks into each waiter's private reverie. Unlike the Plexiglas smoker's structure outside the front door of the River Entrance or the family lounges on the patient wards where parents and other visitors sometimes gather around the microwave to relay their child's medical saga, offer commiseration, and ask for prayer, most of the people in this room are literally screened off. No one is sharing.

I've always been a doer, antsy to get a move on, but there's something about a medical center environment that stifles the compulsion to redeem time through productivity. A canvas bag bulging with reading material and knitting that I tote to Monty's hospital room every day languishes under my seat, and I wonder why I carry the stupid thing around. I haven't cracked a book or magazine in weeks. Even the phone holds no appeal. Periodic coffee runs that I employ to break up long days aren't an option here. A sign in the waiting room warns everyone not to eat or drink in deference to children awaiting surgery.

Who's hungry? Who's thirsty? Who's going to venture out of range for a walk or snack and miss an important summons? The pager tethers us to our seats.

The standard flat screen on the wall of every waiting area, no matter how small, is blessedly absent here, replaced by an aquarium of colored fish, whose wall-eyed existence consists of swimming to and fro in the confines of a their bubbling glassed-in domain. The rhythmic undulation of their tiny tails hypnotizes as I watch them dart through the water and slither back noiselessly so unburdened by existential angst. How I envy them, these aquatic zombies, so graced by ignorance of their limited existence and future, so content to bathe in the moment with no greed for more. I am too cognizant of my own imprisonment in this surgery holding tank, and of my seat time passing like water spilling over the aquarium filter – seconds, minutes, and then hours cascading away. My moments are spent on the edge of my seat. I am too aware of what lies ahead.

I look around the room. The rhythms of normal existence for the people here are partly obliterated by the dearth of natural light, rigid rules, and a pervasive sense that things are out of control. Anyone who's spent any amount of time as an inpatient or even a visitor in a medical facility is familiar with this syndrome. Tunnel-like spaces, so often devoid of any opportunity to see the sun and its movements, the lack of any predictable schedule, and constant intrusions that are part of the hospital routine, all work to sap time of its meaning. Patients and caregivers alike are held hostage by doctor's visits, invasive probes and exams, treatment plans and tests. The chronic underlying dis-ease generated by the disempowering nature of serious illness forces patients and those who stand by them into a state of passivity.

My eyes fall on Monty's friend who sits beside me. Jesse does what he can. He still resides at the Ronald McDonald House, although part of him checked out long ago. Who can blame him? The rigors of Monty's sickness would tax even the most committed of caregivers. It's tough, even for me, and I'm only here once in a blue moon.

"Where have you been all these months?" an older nurse asked one day as I sat by Monty's stretcher waiting for someone to address problems with his IV. I stare into her eyes. Her tone of caring comes tinged with curiosity and anger and includes a manicured finger pointing in my direction. I imagine she thinks that I am a relative.

"This boy has been so alone! So alone! *Where* have you been?"

Monty's medical team posed the same question.

"I'm a friend," I tell them. "I've known Monty since he was eight years old. He was my neighbor. I live in Idaho, about six hours away."

But those medical professional's questions hurt. I know I should have come more often than every few weeks. I wonder how Monty stayed sane during these hellish months by himself in his isolation room. He's nineteen and male and should be at the height of the Ulysses phase of life, when a man climbs mountains, runs races, and proves himself to the world at large. Monty's creative, and, against numerous odds, he was making a life for himself before his diagnosis.

These troubled thoughts are interrupted by the late arrival of Monty's family from the Key Peninsula after almost three hours navigating traffic log jams on the interstate. Jesse and I rise and run to them as if Boone, Lisa, Yvonne, and Daniel are prodigals returning after a lifetime of absence. I am bound to them by shared concern for Monty and memories of Lakeview but little else, yet our differences evaporate when we hug.

Daniel steps forward with familiar fury on this face, and I feel the hurt behind his anger as we sit and talk. He loves his brother. Grandma Yvonne, her voice gravelly, her face lined from years of smoking, is a short, soft-spoken pillar of strength. She raised Monty since he was eleven, and their relationship is solid. Stepmom Lisa is petite and pretty with an open heart of gold, and Boone looks older and heavier than I remember. He has his own brand of quiet strength and has been stepping up to help in various ways. They're accompanied by a neighbor with a digital camera.

Five more hours pass before the electronic alert finally blinks, and the seven of us scurry like a human centipede toward a small windowless room across from the waiting area. Dr. Conrad, his lanky frame clad in green scrubs, stops in the doorway with one foot inside and one out in the hall as if planning a quick exit. A wrinkled paper mask dangles around his neck, and his arms hang limp at his sides as if needing a rest.

Jesse, Monty's family, and I stand in unison, like congregants rising in reverence to a parish priest. We rush toward this middle-aged man and hover like devout worshipers hungering for the Eucharist. We long to hear: "We got it all. The cancer is gone. His future looks bright."

But Dr. Conrad offers none of the assurances or hopeful prognostications we crave.

"The deed is done," he says, his words chosen in accordance with his oath to "first do no harm." Careful phrasing precludes the possibility of annihilating fragile hope or wounding anyone with false optimism. Dr. Conrad is a kind man. His face is furrowed from years on the front lines of the fight against pediatric cancer. It can't be easy.

"Monty is a remarkable person," the noble doctor once commented. "In all my years in medicine, I would have to say that I have never met anyone quite like him."

Because I love Monty, this can only be a compliment, and it soothes my aching heart. Dr. Conrad's recognition of Monty's unique and extraordinary spirit means more to me than he will ever know.

My eyes follow Dr. Conrad as he lumbers away, stoop-shouldered and purposeful, back through the doors to the surgical suite. My yearning for hope seems all the stronger now that the connection to this physician and the promise of health and healing that he represents have disappeared. I swallow salty tears.

The deed is done. There's no cry triumphant.

I am anything but brave.

## Chapter 14

*"No one has greater love than this, to lay down one's life for one's friends."*

— John 15:13

Monty's family and I meander through a coil of hallways and locked barriers into the bowels of Seattle Children Hospital in search of the post-op room where our boy will be brought after discharge from recovery. It's been over nine hours since he went into surgery, and when an orderly finally rolls Monty into the room it's after seven. We rush toward the stretcher and everyone begins talking at once.

Monty's wearing his signature black cowboy hat and a pained expression that intensifies when he's transferred into his bed. We're told that the surgery took so long because of repeated failed attempts to administer an epidural. The freedom from immediate post-op pain so blithely promised by the anesthesiologist will never materialize.

Monty makes weak attempts to be social, but underneath I sense that he's panicky with powerlessness. He wasn't prepared for the enormous cement cast encasing his stump. It's three times as big as his thigh and the weight of it pins him to the bed on his back, unable to move. He complains of something sharp pinching without mercy under the heavy plaster. A thick metal rod with an artificial foot attached to the end protrudes from the bottom of the cast. This contraption was offered as an option when we were first told about the amputation as a way to "have a more normal appearance after surgery." At this point it seems the ultimate travesty – a hideous mockery of what's been lost.

Helium balloons float, their curly ribbons dangling over the bed, and a huge plush octopus from the gift shop sits on the bedside table as if it were a happy occasion – a birthday party. Monty tries to smile for a photo and gives his usual thumbs-up. The neighbor takes a close-up of the stump to document the destruction for well-wishers back home. Everyone tries to be cheerful, but the room is crowded with people and equipment, and the enormity of what's happened and Monty's obvious distress fill what little space is left. There's nothing to say, nothing to talk about. Some head to Starbucks for relief. After a little more than an hour, the visitors head home for the night.

Is there value in describing this scene? Does the recounting of holocausts with their horrifying injuries and heartrending grief cheapen their immense impact like a steady diet of tell-all talk shows, reality television, and lurid tales of loveless sex? Is our interest in medical maladies and hideous cancer stories fueled by fear, voyeurism, and schadenfreude? Is Monty's saga better left untold?

Primo Levi, an Italian Jewish chemist and survivor of the Holocaust, has something to say about this. "A single Anne Frank moves us more than countless others who suffered as she did but whose faces have remained in it the shadows. Perhaps it is better that way. If we were capable of taking in all the suffering of all those people, we would not be able to live."

A relationship with the specific sufferer makes it real. Relationship is at the heart of Christianity, mirrored in Rublev's ancient icon *The Hospitality of Abraham*. This painting depicts the account in Genesis of God's visit to Abraham in the form of three angels representing the trinity. The movement from the Father toward the Son and both Son and Spirit toward the Father shows the intimacy of love. As Henry Nouwen writes: "We come to see with our inner eyes that all engagements in this world can bear fruit only when they take place within this divine circle...the house of perfect love." (*Behold the Beauty of the Lord: Praying with Icons,* p. 20-21)

A direct and personal relationship with the suffering servant, Jesus Christ, is what Christianity is all about. It is not a new and improved version of the Jewish Mishna consisting of dos, don'ts, and dogma. It is not an onerous job. It is not a version of Frederick Nietzsche's take on the meaning of life or Eugene Peterson's adaptation of Nietzsche's quote to define discipleship – "a long obedience in the same direction." It's not something that requires constant toil, vigilance, work, and deprivation.

Intentional movement toward a cognitive understanding of the tenets of Christianity and willful attempts to follow its teachings were a place for me to start in my journey back to God. A change of behavior can sometimes lead to a change of heart. But apologetic arguments, scholarly study, and striving to change my behavior were not enough. It was too easy to become what my Dad used to call a "know-it-all," threatened by anyone or anything that dared to disagree and too easy to make my life all about me. It was too easy to question even God, who I am unable to fully comprehend let alone control or predict.

I came to see that observing Christ on the Cross (the crucifix) and consuming his body and blood in the Eucharist (receiving Him as Catholics do) drew me into a connection with Jesus in purer and more intimate way. I found that through viewing the crucifix, (a wordless symbol which aids identification and connection with Christ's sacrifice), the partaker draws on Jesus's love for all people and His mission to share in their sufferings.

Catholics consume the body and blood of Christ and thus take Him into their very being where He lives on to spread His love to others through His life in them. Like Mother Mary (the Theotokos) we become God bearers, and like Mary, who freely received and freely gave, we receive and give, no matter what the cost. As vulnerable and flawed as humans are, this perfect love removes all fear.

"We're Catholics," says my friend Jeff Helbling. "We're called to enter the circle of suffering of others even when it's scary."

Yet perfect love eludes me on this night in Monty's room. Of course I touch my friend and offer words of comfort and blessing, but my forced cheerfulness seems feeble. I steel my countenance into a self-conscious smile, stifle tears, and look to tasks – offering a drink of water, organizing the bedside table, straightening the covers – anything to squelch the urge to flee. I'm an inept onlooker, an interloper into a private space, so aware of how separate and isolated we all are, our very beings housed in bodies not of our choosing. I am unable to stay in the center of this circle of suffering, unable to will myself to get out of the way and let Jesus work.

Selfless self-donation – the offering of body, soul, and spirit to another without reservations or concern for personal desires and inclinations as Jesus did despite his anguish in the Garden of Gethsemane – runs counter to our primitive drive for survival. I can't know what Monty is experiencing, and I don't want to. Something inside me recoils, and there is a terror and no place to go but back and away. His agony seems a dark eddy, threatening to pull me in. If I get too close that awful pain might pour into me. This is a feeling that's way too familiar from years of dealing with the tragedies I saw on the hospital wards and in the adversities of those close to me.

A coworker in my two person office lived for years gripped in the talons of a noonday demon so intense that nothing could free her.

"Please get out of the car," I tell her one day after driving home from an outing for breakfast and a morning of shopping. We're sitting in the driveway of her house, but she won't move.

"I have to get going. My husband is waiting. I have an appointment to see a friend," I finally blurt out after numerous hints delivered in a softer tone fail to move her. She will not budge.

Excuses tumble from my lips.

Not that I really have pressing business that can't wait. I am weary from months and months of dealing with woman's depression and negative energy, unwilling to go near her vortex of pain and neediness, a black hole of suffering that threatens to suck me in even further.

What is love if not willing the good for another, whatever that requires? Even the biblical King David with all his faults and failures said: "I will not offer burnt offerings to the Lord my God that cost me nothing." (2 Samuel 24).

The things I give to Monty cost so little and come nowhere near sacrifice. He never asks for my meager donations—occasional monetary gifts skimmed from a fat bank account, a few weeks of my physical presence – a pittance really, a smidgeon of my time. He's frank about not wanting yet another stranger, volunteer do-gooder, or commissioned comforter with programmed solace to enter his room but he welcomes me. Our friendship began during another tragic period of his life and is tested true. Perhaps this is the meager gift I have to offer – not words or even time but something intangible, a certain trust that hasn't been broken. This trust can be difficult to find for those who have experienced hurt in the most tender of places.

"You're my Godmother, Mrs. Richards," he tells me on one particularly hard day after the surgery, and my heart breaks with unworthiness.

"I am so proud to be your Godmother, Monty," I tell him with tears in my eyes. I think your Mom is smiling down on us from heaven."

God is something Monty never talks about. Too many food bank proselytizers had forced canned Christianity on him and his tribe when they were just asking for a hand up. Too many Bible thumping crazies selling conditional love poisoned the well. But Monty has retained some rudimentary knowledge of the Christian story from children's programming at the Baptist Church in Lakeview, and he definitely knows where I stand.

"I wouldn't mention any thing about religion to Monty," his stepmother told me one afternoon when we are all feeling the weight of Monty's uncertain future. And I am careful to comply for the most part.

"Preach the gospel..." says Francis of Assisi. "If necessary, use words."

Only Jesse, slacker that he sometimes seems to be, hears the words of St. Francis and takes them to heart. Only Jesse offers himself up, volunteering to sleep on a cot by Monty's bed through the night after the amputation. Jesse suffers *with* Monty, showing the courage to remain by his friend's bedside in his hour of need. His offering is the very definition of compassion and the type of bravery that one would expect from a valiant warrior of his age. I have tremendous admiration for him for that.

As for Monty, he will live a large part of the Ulysses phase of his time on earth wearing a Johnny coat in a hospital room on the 8th floor of the children's cancer unit and later in a travel trailer on the Key Peninsula. He will be discharged from the hospital, to move on the best he can.

This time with only one leg to stand on.

## Chapter 15

*"The best activities are the most useless, because they are done not to accomplish a goal, but merely for their own sake."*

— Aristotle

It's one grey day in May when I cross the narrow bridge by the Purdy Slough and head up the two lane Key Peninsula Highway that winds along the Carr Inlet. Low clouds hover over the water as I motor through mist, snaking through towering old growth spruce and cedar on a slick road that gets darker and narrower by the minute. It's been nine months since Monty's discharge from the hospital, and I'm headed toward his Grandma's house in Home, Washington. I haven't seen Monty for a long time. My visit is long overdue.

I've been to Yvonne's place before, yet the fog gives the road an eerie unfamiliar feel. I scour the thicket for the painted sign that indicates the turn to Home, also known as Lakebay. Signage and landmarks are few and far between on this meandering route, and it's hard to gauge progress. The drive seems to be taking too long.

Monty and I haven't talked much since the amputation. He hasn't called in months. He's stopped answering his phone or responding to texts and all contact has been honed down to occasional brief exchanges on Facebook. Unpaid phone bills, fee disputes, interpersonal issues, and technological glitches with an ever-changing number of cellphone plans are just some of the ongoing explanations offered for this state of affairs.

"There's not much good news to report Mrs. Richards," he offers after one long communication hiatus. "I'm getting used to life with one leg. Do you know any right leg amputees that need brand new shoes? I have a whole stack of shoes for a left foot. I am thinking of advertising on a website."

But Monty's communication blackout doesn't keep the devastating news from reaching across the miles via a Facebook message from his sister in Lakeview.

*I'm sorry I am the one that is telling you this, Mrs. Richards. Monty was transported last night by ambulance to Tacoma General where he was immediately put into an MRI where they found multiple tumors.*

Once again it's time to head west.

I finally spot the small wooden plaque for Home nailed to a tree and turn onto the first paved country lane paralleling the highway. Yvonne's sagging Smurf-colored house sits close to the road surrounded by dense foliage and looks much the same as it did nine years ago. An ancient birdbath is nestled in tall grass in the front yard next to a rusty patio table and two white plastic lawn chairs with seats full of standing water. I swing the car into the dirt driveway and turn off the ignition to sit for a while and collect my thoughts.

The tall trees and undergrowth surrounding the property are veiled in thick mist. The air is muggy, infused with the musty scent of moist soil and wet wood. The world seems muffled and surreal. Except for two stone cherubs bubbling in a fountain by the door, there's nary sign of life. Yvonne's car is gone, and I imagine she and Boone and Lisa are at the diner a half mile down the road where they work. Two cars with flat tires peek out from thick vegetation, and piles of scrap metal, weathered plywood, and various odds and ends gleaned from construction and deconstruction projects over the years lie scattered willy-nilly in the underbrush. I knock on the door of the home and peer through a tiny window into the entryway and beyond to the living room before deciding to pick my way through an overgrown yard toward an old RV out back where Monty has been known to hang out.

Monty's ancient canned-ham style trailer molders in tall weeds, its white metal siding coated with rust and black mold. Its cloudy windows, some cracked and broken, appear to be falling out of their casements. A tattered plastic tarp, held in place with old tires, is draped over the top. This spot, sandwiched between Yvonne's house and a fifth wheel that's home for his dad and stepmother, has long been Monty's private space, a place to retreat. I tap on the door, and Monty calls out in the singsong voice of a game show host.

"Come on...n...n...n... in..."

The light-weight aluminum door creaks and wobbles loose on its hinges as I pull back on its handle. The entire edifice tilts to the right under my weight as I step off a single cinder block stair to make my way inside.

An unplumbed porcelain toilet sits in the corner across from the door. The boy I have come so far to see is lying on a foam mattress on top of a wooden platform that spans the width of the cab at the far end, and I step over magazines and assorted junk to make my way back. Empty pop bottles and food cartons carpet the floor and crunch underfoot. Piles of used and unused medical supplies, stacks of papers, and pill bottles – most of it rubbish from numerous pharmacy runs and hospitalizations – litter every flat surface. There's a funky smell that hard to define. Monty has been living in squalor in this stifling travel trailer for some time – his tall, thin form scrunched into the narrow bed with his computer and vape pipe, where he spends his days huffing himself into a stupor.

"Hi, Mrs. Richards," he states flatly, as if months and months had not passed since we last spoke.

He offers me a seat on a rolling desk chair that's tipped against a built-in desk along one wall, and I disentangle the wheels from various electrical wires and debris to plant myself next to the bed. A system of extension cords connecting hovel to house hang in loops from the ceiling to provide power for a portable heater, camp lamp, and to keep a small refrigerator running. Monty's proud of this setup.

"I have everything I need right here," he says waving his hand as if displaying the grandeur of a custom mansion.

He's hidden his marijuana and prescriptions in a tiny non-working oven next to the bed to deter thieves. The stand-alone toilet (his Dad's contribution to this man cave) was installed to save trips to the bathroom. His computer has thankfully gone dark, sparing us from its noise.

Questions about the difficulties of adjusting to life with one limb are a place to begin. Monty rarely complains, at least to me, but today he is quick to admit that day to day life since the surgery hasn't been easy. The eagerly awaited standard-issue prosthesis from Medicaid, long ago deemed more of a pain than a panacea, gathers dust in the corner by the makeshift commode, its lacquered toes going nowhere. Although well-known for his unusual inventions crafted from ordinary materials around the house, efforts to fashion a silly "peg leg" from a dowel, belt, and tubular bandage proved unworkable, and he's defaulted to crutches. He rarely goes out anymore except for an occasional outing in his brother's car. Jesse's gone back to living with his parents, and he and Monty are no longer speaking. After they left Ronald McDonald House, they severed all connection. Too much togetherness, among other things, shattered the relationship.

Monty spends most days watching horror flicks and reality crime shows and playing games on his laptop. Monthly Social Security disability checks and food stamps are his only income and his contribution to the household. Work is not an option. He has been liberally medicating himself with prescription narcotics and heavy doses of cannabis to address flank pain which has been increasing. Vaping pot takes the edge off.

"These drugs were obtained with a legal permit for medicinal use, even though marijuana is now legal in the State of Washington, Mrs. Richards" he says with pride. "I decided to get a certificate and keep things on the up and up just in case." Monty stores the permit in his wallet and makes a point of showing it to me.

"I've been having trouble lifting this arm," he explains, as he reaches for his vape pipe buried in a tangle of bedclothes.

My spirit sinks when he tells me this, even after reading Chris's email. Impaired movement and increasing pain are both ominous symptoms indicating serious spinal involvement. We don't talk about the trip to Tacoma General and the "multiple tumors."

"The discomfort I'm having in my back is a muscle tear from crutching, and it's affecting my arm," Monty tells me in a matter-of-fact manner as he makes several attempts to lift his arm above his head without success.

"Is that what the doctors say?" I ask, not sure where the answer will take us but not willing to blow the cover off his denial. His elbow points downward despite repeated efforts to lift it above his head. I stare in horror. It's rumored that he's skipped follow-up appointments with his care team in Seattle since the first of the year. I'm not sure his doctors even know about the results of the latest scan or his recent mobility issues.

"Oh Mont, this is not good. How long has this been going on?"

"I have an appointment tomorrow to talk with a surgeon about getting the tumor reamed out," he offers with his particular brand of confident but naïve assurance.

No long discourses this time. He keeps it simple.

"They're going to go in there and clean it out, Mrs. Richards. Then I'll be okay."

My heart races and my eyes brim.

"No crying, Mrs. Richards," he says staring at me, his eyes full of reproach. You know me. Whatever happens, happens. I take what comes."

This I know is true. Monty's ever-resilient nature, evident from the first moment we met, prevents him from becoming mired in dark thoughts for very long. He always moves on.

And I let him.

We jabber about everything and nothing for the rest of the afternoon. Monty entertains me as he always does with fanciful stories, true or not, of his past antics and the scandals and adventures of the people in his community. I learn about bongs and hash oil, superhero films, the gaming world, and the details of dysfunctional social dramas that I would not generally be exposed to in my life as a middle-class woman of a certain age. Frequent breeches of an unwritten code that governs the bartering and sharing of goods and resources for those without much discretionary income stand at the center of every one of these complicated tales. Trust is repeatedly broken, and friends and acquaintances so often prove unreliable. Low expectations help to keep the hurt of many injustices in check. As far as Monty is concerned, the ultimate injustice – the diagnosis of metastatic disease at the age of nineteen – rarely comes up. When it does, he's quick to respond:

"If somebody has to get cancer, it may as well be me."

The words I might say are caught in my throat. They will never find a voice. Monty has never read it, but a passage from the book of Sirach resonates. "Accept whatever happens to you; in periods of humiliation, be patient. For in fire gold is tested and the chosen, in the crucible of humiliation." (Sirach 2: 2-5)

\*\*\*\*\*\*\*\*

The afternoon ticks away, and soon it is past seven. The hours simply evaporated. We followed no agenda during our six-hour gabfest, yet somehow our conversation never lags.

Night eventually falls as it never fails to do. Hunger hits. Monty crutches out to my car for the drive to El Sombrero for Mexican despite the pain in his back that bites with every movement. We sit in a booth and recount memories of other meals we shared over the years. Monty relishes every mouthful of steak fajita after his day of toking and yabbers on and on as he often does, concocting elaborate fanciful tales of the high jinx of his peers and imparting detailed information on numerous topics, most of it of questionable veracity.

"If you leave a tooth in a glass of Coke overnight, it will be dissolved by morning," he says with an air of certainty.

"I doubt that Monty. If Coke was that caustic, wouldn't it eat through your stomach?"

"It's true, Mrs. Richards. There's a top-secret recipe for the stuff that only a few people know. They keep it under lock and key. Whatever's in Coke reacts with calcium to break down the structure of bone."

"You've been nursing your soft drink all night Monty. What's that doing to your bones? Your skeleton isn't going to crumble right here in a booth at El Sombrero is it?"

"This is Pepsi, Mrs. Richards. It's not all pop, just Coke."

"That's an urban legend you read on the internet, Monty, and it isn't true. The boy chatters on and I listen as I always have, struggling to keep my eyes from rolling back into my skull as he offers yet another fantastic story full of wild allegations. It doesn't matter what I say.

As I step outside the car later that evening to accompany Monty to his front door, I look skyward to see the massive trees surrounding Yvonne's place stretching their limbs to the heavens as if in worship. From somewhere in my bank of memories, the words of a Sunday school tune come to mind: "For the beauty of the earth...For the love that from our birth, over and around us lies." The natural world once again descends like a zephyr to soothe my aching mind and awe me with its power to lift my thoughts beyond the horizontal plane.

How easy it is to stay mired in the material world, rushing through time, working because it seems there's no other choice, scrambling for superficial pleasures wherever they can be found. Caught in whirlpools of temporal minutia, niggling away our days, obsessed with trivial pursuits and a never ending series of inevitable problems that pop up like weeds in a wheat field, we slowly spend our lives immersed in controversy, addicted to the titillation of rivalries, scandal, and who's hot and who's not. In the midst of trouble like this boy faces, it can take a special effort in all the madness to stave off the snipping dogs of despair and fear in this valley of tears and to see the joy and beauty in a world torn with so much contention and suffering. It can be so hard to lift our minds and hearts to an unseen God.

Troubling thoughts about the inequitable nature of human adversity that have plagued me for decades once again bob to the surface. Why did eight-year-old Monty, so burdened with the sudden violent loss of his mother, come to ring my doorbell on that October afternoon so many years ago, and why did I see his mother and her love for him and grow to love him myself across time and space despite stark differences in age and back ground? Why do I thrive in my sixties only to see this remarkable boy cut down and denied his dreams?

How did I get from a suburb on Long Island to a dilapidated travel trailer on the Key Peninsula to spend an entire afternoon with a sick boy huffing cannabis oil? The trajectory of life remains mysterious. I'm known for short phone conversations, an inability to sit through a movie, and a strong aversion to mindless chit-chat. I grew up back East in the 50's and 60's, a child of second generation Americans whose parents boarded steerage from the old country. I had never seen the interior of a travel trailer or had exposure to hash oil, vape pens, and the like until this day despite coming of age at the dawning of the *Age of Aquarius*.

I picture myself gazing out at the desert from the window of a client's shack in Christmas Valley, Oregon, in the 1990, ruing the twists of happenstance that brought me to the Oregon

Outback. I glory in the memories of chartreuse light streaking against inky velvet while dog sled mushing in Alaska and in the splendid summer day in August when my friend, Betty Jo, and I of floated down the St. Maries River in inner tubes. I marvel at the good fortune that brought me to the bottom of a coal mine in Wales, and to the birthplace of St. Francis of Assisi. I think of my Grandma Mitzel sailing from her humble home in Aschbach, Austria past the Statue of Liberty before landing at Ellis Island in 1912. Might she have been similarly awed by her fate? Were these happenings part and parcel of a divine plan?

Why things happen or the reason for the existence of any single person in the universe, let alone the meaning of that existence when examined thru the laws of logic, always results in a sigh and a shrug.

I look over at Monty as he gathers his crutches to get out of the car. What do I see in this cancer riddled boy with his scraggly goatee and quirky personality? What about him compels me to drive for hours from Idaho to see him? I watch his thin form swaying as he crutches on one leg through the weeds to reach for the handle of the door of his dilapidated camper. He turns and smiles at me.

"See you tomorrow, Mrs. Richards," he yells lifting one crutch to wave.

It's a moonlit night, and he looks radiant. Beautiful. I wave back.

All questions about productivity aside, this day may have been one where I can truly say:

"For this I was born."

And I am thankful for Monty. I am thankful for this time together.

It will never come again.

## Chapter 16

> "I am too bewildered to hear, too dismayed
> to look.
> My mind reels, shuddering assails me;
> The twilight I yearned for has turned into
> dread."
>
> — Isaiah 21: 3-4

The night passes ever so slowly until daylight finally dawns. My back aches from long hours curled into a narrow love seat in Yvonne's front room. My throat burns from the acrid cigarette haze that hangs in the air. Monty's cat brushes my leg, and I cringe and shush him away. Crumpled street clothes and camper's hair fit my mood. I need coffee.

It's another foggy morning on the peninsula, and the house is quiet. My throat tightens as sober thoughts of what lies ahead float to mind. I yank the covers up to my chin, melt back into the cushy upholstery and close my eyes, consciously trying to relax and drift back into that blissful state between wakefulness and sleep but it's a no-go. The refrigerator motor clicks on. A car zooms by on the dirt road in front of the house. Sensing my overwhelming disgust at his feline overtures, the pesky tabby purrs and eyes me from across the room – twitching his tail in preparation for his next attack. It's time to get up.

Once again I've arrived during one of the pivotal moments in Monty's medical trek without any real planning or forethought. He needs to be examined by his care team in Seattle as soon as possible, and I've been pressed into service to provide transportation.

Monty trudges into the room around eight, bleary-eyed and silent, stump swinging, wincing with every step as he crutches toward the bathroom for a much needed shower. There's a sense of foreboding in the air. Everyone feels it. It's more than worries about Seattle traffic, getting to the clinic at a reasonable hour, or the typical pre-medical appointment jitters. There's no time for idle conversation. No time for breakfast or a second cup of coffee. An invisible muse calls: "Let's move."

Lisa scurries from house to car padding the back seat of the Honda with pillows and blankets and stocking it with the warm soda and the energy drinks Monty is fond of. She packs a suitcase "just in case." The three of us climb into the car for the long drive over the Tacoma Narrows Bridge to the city.

Monty's pain begins to escalate as soon as we turn onto the highway toward Purdy. He can't get comfortable in the cramped quarters of the backseat, and he's vocal about it. Large doses of oral pain medication prescribed from the very beginning of his medical ordeal have lost most of their punch, and it's obvious that he's been relying on marijuana for relief. Forced into a prone position in the back of the Honda without the vape pen for additional support, he starts to lose it.

The frenetic pace of the interstate through Tacoma and Seattle, with its narrow lanes teeming with travelers, never fails to ramp up my anxiety, but on this trip I'm even more on edge. Monty's anguish is contagious and he's begging. Lisa has been doling out pain meds on a schedule, and it's way too soon for the next dose of narcotic. After a protracted back and forth discussion, Lisa relents.

Over an hour later we exit the freeway and begin making our way down 45th Street toward the hospital. The medication kicks in, and we drive in silence, arriving with an hour to spare before the appointment. To our surprise Monty suggests that we stop for something to eat. We speed past the residential roads by Ronald McDonald House as we head back toward a *Papa Johns* in a strip mall by a small park. Jesse, Monty, and I have eaten there before, and it's one place in Seattle that I can find without a map. By the time we get there Monty's zonked.

The pizzeria reeks of pepperoni past its prime, and I suppress the urge to forget about eating. A frantic cook behind the counter informs us that he's working on a backlog of forty-four pizzas. Monty is sleeping in the car so we decide to wait. The harried chef slops together pie after pie, flinging grated cheese everywhere and sloshing sauce onto the floor all while grousing about an assistant who left for a home delivery never to return. He repeatedly apologizes for the fact that order is taking so long and offers to give us the meal at no cost, which is an unexpected blessing. We reluctantly accept.

A half hour later, Lisa and I climb back in the car with our free cheese pizza and three drinks and drive two blocks to a park around the corner. We pull into the parking lot by a sloping sidewalk that leads down to a single picnic bench in the grass by some tennis courts. Monty assures us he can make it down the gentle incline, so Lisa and I run over to set up the meal and scurry back to help our boy hobble to the table and get settled.

An older man with a developmental disability approaches to announce that he is the official greeter for the park. He's a stocky gentleman, a pleasant sort, who's quick to smile and eager for conversation. He rattles on about his job, which includes gabbing with visitors, emptying trash, and keeping the tennis courts clear of leaves and debris. We offer him a slice of pizza.

But lunch is over before anyone takes a bite. Monty moans and folds over the wooden picnic bench pleading for our help. Something is horribly wrong, and without warning the pain has turned to agony. The trip from the parking lot was a tipping point. We've jumped the shark. The three of us are stuck at the bottom of a hill, and there's no way Monty can crutch back to the car.

But Lisa and I don't have time to panic. The universe delivers at the precise moment of need before we even think to ask. A green pick-up with a *City Parks* logo pulls onto the grass and stops right beside the table as if on cue and an angel sans wings in the form of a park ranger, who just happened to swing by to check on the greeter, exits the cab. After contacting his dispatcher, the two men hoist the wailing boy into the front seat of the truck for the short trip to the parking lot.

Minutes later Lisa and I wheel Monty through the doors of the Seattle Children's clinic entrance, where he screams and falls out of the wheelchair onto a long bench.

"We need a stretcher," I tell the security personnel at the front desk, and a uniformed guard picks up a phone. An alert goes over loud speakers, and in seconds a moving mass of men and women flock to our aid like a gaggle of crazed birds in white lab coats swooping down on their prey. They rush toward Monty out of nowhere rolling carts of supplies and various machines and barking questions. They whisk our boy to the emergency room where more geese in white garb gather.

"This boy has a reason to be in pain," one doctor comments as Monty wails on the exam table surrounded by a score of medical professionals who all seem to be wringing their hands. Everyone is concerned about the extra dose of pain medication he has on board. None of these professionals seems to know how to proceed.

Lisa and I watch from the doorway of the emergency exam room. Dr. Conrad rushes up, and the three of us stand together in the back. The tall doctor looks down into our eyes with recognition, and we exchange a few words. He stares at Monty writhing on the cot surrounded by the medical team. Lisa and I huddle together, backs to the wall of the ER – helpless...paralyzed.

The only things moving are our tears.

## Chapter 17

*"The heart was made to be broken."*

— Oscar Wilde

The phone by the bed in my brother-in-law's guest room startles me awake. Lisa's voice cracks as she relays the news. Much as I suspected, the tumor's growth is pressing on Monty's spinal cord and compromising his ability to move his arm. Once this dire situation was documented by MRI, doctor's rushed him to surgery. I am already back on the road to the hospital. It's 4 a.m.

Lisa and I cling to each other as we sit in the waiting room outside the surgical suite hours later. We cry with a family grieving for their dying six-month old child – parents and grandparents in the throes of one of the most horrible of all losses. Their baby seemed healthy yesterday but a virulent virus attacked and now he is on life support. Their sobs tear us apart, and there's no place to retreat. And then it is our turn.

"We cleared the tumor around the cord, but it's just a stop-gap measure," the surgeon tells us, his middle-aged eyes brimming sorrow. "Our team inserted a metal rod to support his spine, but your boy is full of cancer and the tumors will continue to grow."

When we see Monty hours later, he is heavily sedated in intensive care and in so much pain that bumping against his bed causes him to cry out. Four days later doctors will clear him to move back to his regular room on the eighth floor, where he will continues to struggle to adjust to the hardware holding his spine together. Within one week the neurosurgeon's predictions after the surgery will begin to come true. Monty notices decreased feeling and motion in his leg and right arm. He is having trouble emptying his bladder. He's losing control of his body.

Lisa and I take turns by the bedside. The curtains of our boy's glass cell are drawn to block the curious from peering in through the heavy sliding door. Hordes of medical specialists bustle in and out of the room day and night. They enter with computers, their scanners, and bar-coded syringes in zip-lock bags, popping capsules into pleated paper cups from blister packs with hands covered in latex. They duck in to silence the cacophony of beeping IV machines and oxygen sensors that threaten our sanity day and night, or slip through the sliding door to throw a package of giant baby-wipes on the bed for Monty's so-called bath. But there's nothing they can do to stop the cancer now.

The flat screen on the wall across from Monty's bed glows in the dark, spewing forth its testimony to the immense pleasures the world affords, and I stifle the urge to silence its offerings. Families laugh and frolic with Mickey and his gang in the "happiest place on earth" with "When You Wish Upon A Star" playing in the background. Limber athletes scurry down soccer fields reveling in their amazing athleticism and youthful vigor. Travel ads flash gorgeous models in bikinis sunning by a pool in the tropics, eating sushi, drinking Mai Tais and making merry. A handsome actor beams with pride as he speeds along in a new Ford pickup with a blonde cutie riding shotgun. *Dupont* brashly touts the "miracle of science," but there is no miracle here. Despite testimonies advertising their power, Gold Mastercards are worthless in the face of metastatic cancer. No magic kingdom, colored ribbon or hope for a cure for this young man.

Monty seems more open to comment on his situation after this major setback and the serious pain that has resulted. He had an episode in ICU one night where he couldn't catch a breathe, and it was so terrifying that he continues to insist on wearing a nasal cannula " just in case," even though the oxygen has been turned off for days. He talks about dying.

"I realize I don't have much time left Mrs. Richards."

"None of know how much time we have, Monty. We just take life one day at a time."

"Yeah, but I thought I was dying the other night. I really got scared. I didn't think I was going to make it."

"I'm so glad you are okay," I tell him, but don't say much else. It seems important for me to let him lead the conversation on this topic.

"I'll never have my own house," he says wistfully as yet another real estate show host blathers on about his latest beach front listing. The camera pans over the interior of a spectacular property on the California Coast zeroing in on an impeccably dressed couple out for a day of house hunting. They whine about one of the four bathrooms being too small and bicker about the floor-plan and the color of the walls in the master bedroom. Monty looks at me, and his immense sorrow flows my way.

"I wish I had to worry about those kinds of things. I had plans, Mrs. Richards, to buy my own place, to get married someday, and have my own family. Some of the stuff people gripe about is so stupid"

Monty's creative job in the sheet metal shop, playing football with his brother, having children of his own – his dreams for the future have all been stamped void. "No wonder the word cancer and cancel look so similar," Amy Krouse Roenthal wrote after being diagnosed with ovarian cancer at the age of forty-nine and seeing her plans and hopes for the future disappear. Things have been lost that will never be found. Things have gone wrong that can never be made right.

Other casualties also came with his diagnosis – the loss of privacy, autonomy, and human dignity – resulting from of the draconian measures required for treatment of cancer and the hideous side effects of those treatments. Amidst this sterile, state of the art facility immersed in techno-scientific prattle, patients are often objectified. Modern medicine increasingly dehumanizes them by failing to see that each person is more than a sum of his or her parts. Medical personnel so often seem to focus exclusively on testing and treating organ systems, addressing symptoms and complaints with cocktails of chemicals administered according to standard policies. They too often fail to consider the whole individual in all his or her complexity. Scripted responses, so infuriatingly disingenuous, are used to deal with the complex emotions of anger and fear that are sure to come.

"We won't tolerate that kind of behavior," said one clueless "pain specialist" when Monty punched the side rail of his bed in frustration.

Is this kind of scripted wording really the standard of care and compassion? Are we becoming human robots, offering programmed responses to even the most heartfelt emotions? Is it so hard to acknowledge the hurt and frustration here?

I cringe remembering confrontations with the pain team and their condescending approach – a flock of white coated authoritarians with clip boards marching with military precision down the hallways, into and out of patient rooms, in lockstep, heels clicking. I imagined them ensconced in pristine meeting rooms around a conference table with their lattes and laptops discussing the "science" of pain management and making decisions per protocols written in stone – never listening or taking the time to offer a dose of their time, a touch of tenderness, or a trial of talk therapy. Chemical solutions are their only prescription. Pills, potions, and ice packs seem the only things offered for pain of every kind. They could not be moved.

"They're used to treating little kids," Monty complained over and over. "They don't know what to do with adults."

I'm not sure this was true, but it is a fact that each medical specialty team – the orthopedists, oncologists, radiologists, etc.– looks only at their own area of concern and punts to the pain pundits when asked to address issues of suffering of every kind, and that sometimes makes me want to scream.

Standing in a hallway outside of Monty's room one day, I glance up to see a laminated sign with a list of color coded emergencies. In the old days we had "Code Blue" to alert staff of a cardiac arrest, and "Code Red" for a fire, but today the list has expanded to cover earthquakes and other weather extremes, bomb threats, hazardous spills, abductions and lockdowns. There's even a code for a parental meltdown, a "Code Brown," which I hear broadcast over the public address system one day. I don't know the reason, but I imagine a young father watching his little son's misery, finally snapping and going postal in the ICU. He's ballistic in the face of his powerlessness to influence the medical machine that forges ahead on the basis of science and objective data without restraint, very often overlooking, or even dismissing, the emotional distress that comes with a medical crisis. I could be that parent.

My physician friend, Rick, once noted that the most valuable tool for medical practitioners is listening to the patient's story. Few people's stories fit into a printed form, a number scale, or a drop down screen. The accumulation of objective data (and all data is objective), is and always will be incapable of addressing the subjective nature and reality of personal experience. Albert Einstein noted that "Not everything that can be counted counts and not everything that counts can be counted." Is it so hard to admit the frequent impotence of information and science and touch the patient and family with a simple token of one's own humanity? During all my time at Monty's bedside, I saw only one man who was able to do that.

"Why does this kind of thing happen to anyone?" remarks Dr. Luz, a resident on the oncology team as we stand together outside Monty's hospital room discussing the ever advancing growth of the tumor eating into his spine. Dr. Luz peers through the thick lenses of his glasses into Monty's dark cell with faraway eyes as if looking to rise above time and place. He dares to enter into his patient's experience and expose his own existential angst. For a medical professional to go beyond the scientific banter, acknowledge suffering, and even broach the question of "why" is *so* rare. These few words spoken outside the standard format of routine rounds touch me and provide a healing salve in this antiseptic place. Dr. Luz's comment shines in this darkness. It's so ironic that his name in Spanish means light.

Perhaps everyone asks "why?" even if not aloud. It comes up at some point in every tragedy, compelling the grieving to find someone or something to blame. My Grandpa's wife believed his demise was caused by the Rice Krispies he'd consumed the morning of his heart attack. Uncle Dick credited his jaw cancer to his frequent use of black pepper despite the fact that he'd been smoking two packs of Pall Malls every day since he was fifteen. But when a young person is stricken, the question is more of a wail of anguish from somewhere deep within.

"Why Monty?" his brother, Daniel, asks dolefully. "Of all of us, Monty is the good one – never took dope, never did anything." Daniel's plea for answers is suspended in amber, voicing the grief of generation after generation of Jobs and their loved ones through the ages.

"It's God's perfect will, Janet – His Divine care and guidance over his creatures," says one well-meaning Christian friend. "Jesus asked the Pharisees if it was the blind man or his parents that sinned to cause the blindness and Jesus told them that it happened so the works of God might be displayed in him."

"Thanks Penny," I say, but I bristle at these words that seem so empty and mean in the midst of my boy's pain, even as I hold onto their truth. I'm limited by my humanity, pinned as I am to this mortal coil without the ability to understand. It hurts to hear about God's weaving or conjectures about His view from the other side of the tapestry of a life. I recoil when others talk of plans God has to make it all good in the end as if they have privileged knowledge of the working of the mind of the Creator.

But, even in this hurt, I cannot let go of God. I retreat to the cloud of "unknowing" and rest my weary mind in the soft amorphous folds of blind faith. I hope for something I cannot see, because the alternative is too awful. I have to believe in a better plan. A divinely devised design that's so good that it's beyond what anyone can wish for or even imagine.

And I believe in the mystery of how two souls come together. Who can explain why we like some individuals and not others or why some people become major players in our lives?

"Monty manipulates you, Mom," I hear my children say over and over, harking back to the days in Lakeview, when they realized that I let Monty get away with more than I did for my own offspring.

"You aren't seeing him for what he is. You idolize him."

"Monty's had some hard breaks," I tell them, hoping for some compassion, but I know where they are coming from. Although Monty has high ideals, he's just like every other human on the planet and makes mistakes. Although he continues to seek out COPS and other shows where the bad guys get their comeuppance and often preaches about the morality of right and wrong, he sometimes doesn't pay his fines or his phone bill. Once he accidentally sped off with the gas tank nozzle still stuck in his car and, instead of offering restitution for repairs to the pump, vowed to avoid that station for the rest of his life. It's possible that many of the more inventive stories about his childhood may have been concocted to gain sympathy. Sometimes I think he actually believed they happened. Survival can call for drastic measures. It can force us to defend our identity and to fabricate fiction about who we are and who we want to be.

Monty liked to call himself a *Brony*, a regular dude, a young male fan of *My Little Pony* cartoons. Most *Bronies* are friendly teenagers and young adults that simply aren't afraid to admit that they enjoy a show with a moral theme that is interesting, colorful, and fun. The ponies look out for each other. When one pony loses her tail in a freak accident, others gather round to offer snippets of their own tail hair to help restore their friend's confidence. Story elements of the series include honesty, kindness, laughter, generosity, loyalty, and magic against evil, and touch on universal themes that transcend age and gender. I think of *Bronies* as idealists, hoping for a kinder, gentler future for the world. Monty's favorite *My Little Pony* might be Rainbow Dash, who could not abandon her friends for her own heart's desire, who had power to control the weather, and both the self-confidence and the will to win.

I was fortunate to find a Rainbow Dash balloon at Rosauers in Moscow, and I gave it to Monty on one of my visits. He kept the flattened Mylar long after the helium had gone out. The Bible describes the rainbow as a symbol of hope given by God to Noah after the flood. Hope is defined as the feeling that what is wanted can be had. It has an element of trust that some unseen good will materialize, that something better will come. "For who hopes for what they already have?" (Romans 8:24)

Hope is faith. A faith in good.

And all that is good comes from God and is God.

"Our hearts are restless until we rest in Him." (Augustine)

# Chapter 18

> "Sorrow comes as in a circle
> And cannot be rolled up like a mat."
>
> Chinese poetry Chi/in Chia
> "To My Wife"

It's grief, this pressure behind my eyes and the tightness in my throat, as I trudge along to my car after a long day at Monty's bedside. My legs and feet tingle and ache as I slump along a cement walkway strewn with wheelchairs to the top level parking lot toting a cloth bag filled with empty water bottles and sick room ephemera. Young medical workers speed by, reinforcing just how old and exhausted I am. The orange lanyard of the badge identifying me as an official caregiver bobs on my chest as I plod along – a constant reminder of my role, an outward declaration to those I meet that someone I love is sick.

Fellow caregivers also slump along toward the parking lot, their status also broadcast by the color of their neck-wear. Some glance over to exchange wordless empathy. The serious bodily dysfunctions that brought each of us to a children's hospital are as varied as the human species. Each illness charts its own course, carrying those who serve at the bedside on unique and separate journeys.

A few people connect to share medical anecdotes with words full of veiled anger and wistful hope, but most are silent. Many ask for prayers – the parents of a young volleyball champ who injured her spinal cord in a bicycle accident, a young mother caring for her fourteen-month-old son with life threatening birth defects who permanently resides in ICU, and so many others who have children struggling with cancers of every ilk. We're all strangers on speeding trains traveling on parallel tracks. The route to a hoped-for cure is pocked with potholes, detours, and delays, and defies prediction.

The families of hospitalized children frequently languish for hours and days, fused to uncomfortable acrylic chairs in environments essentially devoid of natural light. Some veg out, eyes dull, too tired to do anything but stare at the talking heads droning drivel on the flat-screen television attached to the wall of each and every patient cell and waiting room. Serious illness, like poverty, subjects loved ones and those they care for to the tyranny of the moment. Some parents remain silent in their child's isolation room, too sapped to socialize. Many aspects of illness and the hospital experience work to impede community building and drain a person of strength to do anything but cope. Constructing meaningful sentences takes energy.

Most days Lisa and I are planted by Monty's bed like sentries waiting for the next IV alarm to scream for attention, distressing symptom to pop up, or a team of white coats to descend with more opinions, plans, and prognostications that seems so imperative to hear. Monty's step mom is younger and more energetic, but anticipatory tension devours both of us. The routines of daily living – bathing, eating, sleeping, and finding clean clothes – require planning, and most days the strength just isn't there. Lisa has a room at RMH, so she can stay with Monty while he recovers from the surgery. She gives him backrubs and foot massages, and is a gentle blessing to her stepson. I sometimes sleep at RMH, too, but tonight I'm heading home to my brother-in-law's house in Enumclaw for a night's respite.

Breaking out of the artificial atmosphere of the hospital with its florescent lighting and polished floors into the sunny natural world always exalts my spirit after a long day inside. My senses keen as fresh air and sunshine hit my face – so brilliant and uplifting compared to the cold glass, and polystyrene laminate world I just left. Blue sky, whip cream clouds, and rustling trees soothe and bless – no poisonous potions flowing through plastic, no alien machines beeping torture, no bureaucratic tyranny and invasive technology. Freedom is at hand. I picture myself in the porch swing on Jane's deck outback viewing the rows of raspberry bushes in Bruce's garden and breathing in the fresh evening air with Mount Rainier as a backdrop.

Yet it hurts to think that this glorious world twirls on as Monty and other ailing children languish in cloistered units, their daily tedium broken only by transport to yet one more medical procedure via a tortuous tangle of windowless cubicles and hallways. I am free to leave.

I finally make it across the busy parking lot, fling my weary carcass into the car, and melt into its warm seat. I crack both windows wide to clear the air, pop a disc into the CD player, and take a sip of lukewarm water from a bottle in the cup holder on the dash. A stuttering sigh escapes with one deep breath as I turn the key to start the engine and adjust the air conditioner.

The ever-present urban congestion bears down once again as I merge into a stream of harried commuters bent on getting home. Even the pleasure of my release from my responsibilities at the bedside is initially lost to the demands of highway vigilance.

Murky thoughts flutter down as I sit in my car at a traffic light. Melancholy vapors swoop out of nowhere these days like an inexplicable murmuration of starlings, undulating and unrelenting. A limber skateboarder sashays with grace down a tree-lined sidewalk, and bikers pedal past, healthy thighs pumping as they weave between the cars inching forward on a city street that has become parking lot. Tattooed teens with sagging pants sulk on busy street corners waiting for the light to change. I stare at every one of them with bitter envy. Don't they realize the gift they have been given?

Deep breaths help to blow away the dastardly demons of depression, and the dark starlings of despair scatter and flee. Familiar Catholic favorites play through the car's speakers, soothing my aching soul and helping me decompress. These are the same songs I've played over the many months, coming and going, and I let their words and melodies, like balm, wash over me. Singing nuns break into *Kyrie Eleison*, "Lord have mercy." The coiled muscles in my neck and back soften as I pray along with them.

"*Ave Maria, Gratsi a Plena....*" Oh for some of the grace poured down from heaven for Mary. In my hour of darkness, mother Mary, the God Bearer, comes to me just as she came to me when I first felt the call to Catholicism during an icon writing workshop. She comes to me as she has to so many others – speaking words of wisdom. Mary stood at the foot of her son's cross. She understands.

And I hear Jesus's words from his sermon on the mount as I race down a two lane road in the dark toward Bruce and Jane's house in Enumclaw.

"Blessed are the poor in spirit for theirs is the kingdom of heaven. Blessed are those who mourn, for they shall be comforted." (Matthew 5:3-4)) I am not alone.

It's close to 10 p.m. when I finally pull into the driveway of my resting place for the night. My sister-in-law runs out in her nightgown to greet me with a holy kiss. I lay my burdens down until they are light enough for sleep.

The orange lanyard hangs limp on a chair by the bedside until the dawning of the next day...a day that will come too soon.

## Chapter 19

One afternoon while Monty's sleeping, I take the opportunity to head downstairs for a cool drink at the Starbucks on the third floor. As noted, Frappuccino's have replaced most of my meals, and I'm hungry. Grande with whipped cream in hand, I meander down the hall in search of the "phone zone" by the front door – one of the only places in the hospital where visitors can find cell reception.

In contrast to the bright sixth and seventh floors with their shared atrium, skylights, and wide corridors bustling with families headed to clinic appointments, the gift shop, or the giant cafeteria, the third floor hallway has a low ceiling and seems tunnel-like and essentially deserted. *Perhaps the weight of suffering endured above compressed the entire building to reduce level three to this narrow passageway*, I think as I shuffle through the gloomy space toward a bank of chairs by the entrance. I plop down in one in the corner to dial my husband for his daily update. No answer.

People stream by as I wilt into a Bauhaus-style chair covered in orange vinyl and proceed to suck on the straw of my icy drink, trying not to think. Most people come to this hotspot to take care of business and/or fill friends and family in on the breaking news of their child's progress. A young couple holds hands as they take turns talking into their cell phone. Their five-month-old baby is in ICU on life support. He was fine yesterday but woke up with a fever. I can't help overhearing their conversation. Their sadness oozes my way.

I've been told that a modern version of a hospital chapel is located somewhere in this area, so I head back toward the Starbucks to begin my search. A small sign for the "Pastoral Care Center" tucked into a dimly lit alcove across from the security desk catches my eye. This obscure location is disheartening, and that familiar hoary troll lets loose with a snarky thought: *The authors of the psalms looked to the hills from whence their help came, but this center for spiritual comfort is crunched into a crack in a valley, scooped out of the wall along a dimy passageway, and easy to miss.* My expectations are low.

The alcove has two doors. To the left lies the locked counseling office, to the right the "meditation room," open 24-7. I move toward the right into a circular room carpeted in beige and ringed with rows of upholstered chairs. Several framed pictures adorn the walls: a bright mandala and plain metal cross. A handful of religious artifacts from various faith traditions and a statue of Buddha are crammed into a glassed-in case to pay homage to the god of religious diversity. Sunlight streams through tall aluminum windows partially obscured by four stained glass panels from the original turn-of-the-century hospital building. The glass eyes of an angel clad in white robes glare at me from one of the windows as if sensing my apostasy.

Over caffeinated and underfed, I pace and ponder as the lump in my throat grows. The silence and solitude of this space feel like chain mail, constricting and heavy, anchoring me to my sadness. My mind scrambles for some type of solace.

A twig wreath covered with strands of colored ribbon rests on an easel in one corner, and I tie on a red for Monty with hope that some kind of action will lift my funk. Two hefty bound books lie open on a circular table under one window, their pages inked with handwritten prayers for sick children. Both volumes are almost full – so many children in these holy books are already dead, so many prayers unanswered. I hastily add an entry for the one I love.

The ribbons, the tomes of unrequited pleas to God scrawled on tear stained parchment, and the reams of grief literature offering pedantic advice for the problem of human pain and sadness seem like so much pop psychology. I feel myself sinking lower.

This meditation room seems a patronizing parody of chapels of the past – a token to a conglomeration of metaphysical gods, a shrine to a sanitized version of politically correct "spirituality." There is no focal point, no crucifix or Holy Icons with illuminated faces. There's nothing to draw me toward transcendence or break the tethers to this earthly plane of tears. The space seems yet another waiting room, albeit one with antique windows in dazzling hues hung on chains from the casements, a few museum pieces behind glass, a shelf of dusty books, stacks of pamphlets on grief, and a panoramic view of the parking lot.

Despite its perceived shortcomings, I return to the pastoral care center because there seems no place else to go. I spend an hour one afternoon unloading on a Unitarian Minister and his tender Catholic cohort until I feel worn out from spent emotion. These men have seen it all – the immense suffering of children and those who love them and yet still have the fortitude to listen. I go back to join hands with family members and caregivers from various cultures at a mass delivered by a palsied priest stumbling through the liturgy in phonetic Spanish and once to sit in the empty chapel to pray and play a few hymns on the piano. Each time I drag the heavy knowledge of my powerlessness and the weight of my own mortality back to the cancer ward no more comforted than when I first arrived.

Perhaps this emptiness is a rite of passage for those who grieve. So many find themselves in this void – the atheists, agnostics, and secular humanists of the world, seeking without finding, and believers like me who are in the midst of a dark night of the soul. The pious wax poetic about ancient scriptures and holy experiences and traditions, but some seekers feel and know nothing. Religious discourse so often seems like so much psychological pap aimed at helping the hurting get through the moment of acute pain – a mental exercise that doesn't last...an "opiate of the people" Many look for a solution to suffering in nirvana (translated from Sanskrit as "the absence of breath") and in all sorts of places. But the breath of life is presence, and the spirit of God so often feels absent.

People reject religion for all kinds of reasons, but often because it seems a negation of their pleasure and happiness, a privation. The cross remains empty of any depiction of the suffering body of Jesus in so many Christian houses of worship because viewing agony on an instrument of torture seems gruesome. Why not focus on the glorious resurrection? But I find a certain comfort in identification with Christ's selfless suffering and servanthood and the ultimate joy of pain's redemption.

Deacon Tom at the Spiritual Counseling Center compares the cancer experience to the Stations of the Cross, and there I find some peace. This is a Catholic tradition of which my family is familiar. We enacted the fourteen scenes of the events leading up to Christ's Crucifixion and death with our Catholic friends every Good Friday, even when we were practicing Protestants. Art depicting the Stations can be found on the walls of most Roman Catholic churches. Meditating on these is at the heart of Catholic Christianity.

The Stations remind me of a passage from Cardinal Bernardin's *Stations of the Cross* by Eugene Kennedy. It describes Jesus's cry from the cross as recorded in the gospels of Mathew and Mark. "My God, my God, why have you forsaken me?"

"But Jesus' lonely shout is...but a plaint for all the rejection, hurt, and separation of all humans...all the sorrows of time, all the bloodied hands gripping iron bars, all the arms bearing wasted and dying children, all the backs bend and scarred by unjust punishments, all the terrified eyes glimpsed as boxcar doors slide shut, all the sweet-faced youth stunned into blank staring death on muddy fields, all those taken down by heartbreak, all those crying against the sky for losses too great to bear or too small to name, all those whose gifts were never opened, and all those denied even a taste of the battered bittersweet glory of being human – for all these Jesus intones his lament in a desperate call from the cross that finished his Father's work by braiding our sorrow into his own."

I thank Deacon Tom for his suggestion to walk my way through the Stations of the Cross and am grateful to him for the peace it bought me.

And I thank God for Catholicism.

# Chapter 20

*"And another regrettable thing about death*
*Is the ceasing of your own brand of magic*
*Which took a whole life to develop and*
*market –*
*The quips, the witticisms, the slant*
*adjusted to a few,*
*Those loved ones nearest the lip of the*
*stage...."*

— John Updike, Perfection Wasted

The year is 1963, and the campers in our unit at Blue Bay Girl Scout Camp are huddled around the campfire in early evening for a sing-a-long. The fire pit glows in the center of a clearing near a cliff overlooking the beachfront along Gardner's bay in East Hampton. Salty smells waft our way as an evening breeze drifts in from the Atlantic sending clouds of smoke toward us, stinging our eyes. There's a chill in the air and campers huddle for warmth, mesmerized by the tongues of flame licking the logs and sparks crackling up and out into inky darkness. We're thirteen and used to each other's closeness, as yet unaware of the concept of personal space.

My four friends and I look like clones in our dusty *Keds*, cutoffs, and camp shirts, our teenage bodies tanned and fit from a summer outdoors, riding our bikes around the streets of the Long Island town on the edge of Queens that we call home. Keddy Ann, Susan, Marjorie, Nancy, and I have known each other since we were seven-years-old students in Miss Palmer's second grade class at Floral Park Bellerose Elementary. We giggled and gallivanted our way through years of grade school recesses, scout meetings, raucous pajama parties with dancing in the streets, and long shifts after school shelf reading for Mrs. Koch as library pages at the Floral Park Public library. We share memories of the major events of our childhood – Alan Shepard's ground breaking travels into space, the assassination of President Kennedy, the Beatles at Shea Stadium, and our fifth grade class trekking through the tunnel under the Long Island Railroad to watch Nixon stumping on a platform in front of the Bellerose Theatre.

How can we forget the camp songs stamped into our gray matter by constant repetition on long bus rides down the center of Long Island, belting out *Mrs. Murphy's Chowder* and *One Hundred Bottles Of Beer On The Wall* in unison as we traveled to our summer camp getaway in Hamptons. How innocent we were in our privileged American middle-class life. Our parents loved and provided for us. Solid expectations and social boundaries gave the illusion of security and promise. Our joy in the present was boundless – a certainty, however fleeting, that all was right and would always be right with the world.

As we gather around the campfire on that glorious evening in 1963 our juvenile voices peal into the night singing in round: "*Make new friends but keep the old. One is silver and the other's gold.*" In truth our thoughts don't include images of anything growing old or imaginations of any kind of loss that the future might hold. None of us have ever known want.

I come from humble stock. My mother's mother, Mitzel, grew up on a farm in rural Austria, and her husband reportedly left Germany at the age of fourteen to sail around the world. They both arrived on America's shores with little in the way of possessions or money. The population of New York City had been doubling every decade at that time, and many buildings previously considered single family dwellings had been divided into multiple living spaces called tenements. These apartments were often poorly lit and lacked plumbing and adequate ventilation. My mother was born in a tenement and lived there with her parents for the first six years of her life. My father's father was a janitor, and his family lived in a two bedroom apartment in Queens. But things had changed by the time I was born. The Navy sent my father to the University of Wisconsin to obtain a degree in engineering, and he later became the vice president of a national company. My seafaring grandpa became a tug boat captain in New York City Harbor and was savvy enough to buy stock in Exon Mobile. My parents helped me through college, and I spent a decade working as a nurse until I married my college sweetheart who just happened to become a doctor. For reasons I cannot fathom, I have been spared a life of poverty in every sense of the word. Not so for the majority of the people in the world.

We are "just a vapor that is here for a short while and then vanishes," says the apostle James (James 4:14), and my friends and I now see that we are closer to the end than the beginning. In what seems like the time it took for an ocean wave to wash ashore and ebb back from whence it came, we find ourselves entering our dotage. Over half a century after that evening around the fire pit, the five of us, sixty-six years old and counting, meet again. We have been graced with long life.

A photo taken outside a restaurant in Wimberly, Texas, documents our reunion in 2016. It shows us in all our late middle aged glory, melted and melting versions of our teenage selves, bodies more lumpy than lean and lithe, lines of love, laughter, and loss etched into weathered faces. Nine marriages, six divorces, seven children, and fourteen grandchildren later, we linger over lunch on the sunny patio surrounded by myrtle trees along a river on a spring afternoon. Stories shared around this table tell of victory, defeat, and regret in the process of coming of age in the late 60's – the drugs, the sexual awakening, Woodstock, Vietnam, motherhood, and loss all filtered through the colored lens of our shared history.

Experiences, like the Atlantic buffeting the rocks of the jetty that stretches toward open sea by Blue Bay Girl Scout Camp, have softened us and furrowed deep – Agent Orange, infertility, mental illness, the betrayal of a spouse, and the death of our nephews. We see how these have shaped us, and we embrace what they reveal.

We laugh into the wee hours of the night. Who else but childhood friends will remember the time when a bird pooped on the slice of watermelon you were eating or recall Pastor Dietrich's ranting screeds on the evil and the eternal repercussions of tipping our heads back too far when partaking of the fruit of the vine during communion? Who else can share the memory of the bright red beginner's dictionary that Mrs. Palmer gave to every child in her second grade classroom and how that book changed our lives.

The privilege of seeing this rich tapestry of our divergent paths at our reunion overwhelms me. Oh, how I ache for Monty to know a moment like this – to be able to look back on such a lavish, long life. For whatever reason, he has been denied what I far too often take for granted.

For whatever reason he has been set, instead, on the fast track to death.

## Chapter 21

*"Today I think that if for no other reason than that an Auschwitz existed, no one in our age should speak of Providence."*

— Primo Levi

The bedroom is pitch black, and the air still and silent when I rouse from deep sleep on a balmy August night. My husband's working out of town, and I'm alone in the house except for our Border Collie mutt, Sophie, splayed in deep slumber on her doggie bed in the corner of the bedroom. I open my eyes long enough to squint at the digital clock. It's 2 a.m.

Consciousness has arrived unbidden, and I'm unwilling to accept its dawn. I squirm like a fryer on a spit adjusting and readjusting the pillows and blankets, alternately too hot and then too cold before finally realizing that all efforts to ease back to the land of nod are futile. Fumbling for the lamp switch, I swing my legs over the side of the bed and hoist my leaden body from its percale cocoon.

There's no yapping cockapoo in the yard next door or soul jarring down beat of heavy rock reverberating from a late-night kegger in the duplex at the bottom of the hill below our house to blame for this state of wakefulness. No roadsters drag racing or semis with air brakes barreling down 95 on this summer night. Not even the crickets are croaking.

Eyes at half-mast, I sit on the side of the bed and glance at the wall across the way. In an instant I am wide awake. Two blurry letters, each a foot tall, suddenly appear as if shining from a celestial projector. They shimmer in neon white, their eerie glow mesmerizing me into a stupor as I struggle to comprehend. Minutes go by before they disappear as quickly as they came. Two simple letters written in light at 2 a.m. on a bedroom wall in Moscow, Idaho. The word they spelled is "DO."

"You need to go see Monty, Mom," my oldest daughter, says one evening during one of our phone conversations. "I'm sure he wants to see you. You might be sorry if you don't go."

My girl was in college during the time Monty lived in Lakeview. She remembers meeting him only once, but she knows I love him.

"It's such a long drive, and I'm not sure I am up for it," I say already mentally listing a long litany of excuses. "As far as I know, Monty's doing fine. He's at home under his stepmother's most excellent care. I just talked to him yesterday."

"Go Mom. Just Go. I know you'll be glad you did."

No instructions written in light on the wall this time, just a strong willed daughter with a type-A personality and a history of demonstrating unrelenting persistence when faced with the word "no."

"Maybe I'll call," I say, hoping my kid will back off. "I want to make sure he's up for a visit and wants me to come. He hasn't been contacting me lately. I don't want to be a pest."

"You know Mom, I don't think he is going to tell you that he wants you to come. It's not going to happen."

Perhaps I don't want to see how Monty's health has deteriorated. Perhaps I don't want to be faced with his suffering or to be there when he dies. Perhaps I am afraid. Am I waiting for some kind of message on the bedroom wall?

The expression "the handwriting is on the wall" comes from an ancient Old Testament story recorded in Chapter 5 of the book of Daniel. The parable begins in the dining hall of King Belshazzar's mansion, where the Babylonian monarch is hosting a feast for his lords, princes, wives, and concubines. The king offers these guests choice foods and special wines served in sacred gold and silver goblets that were stolen from the temple in Jerusalem by his father, King Nebuchadnezzar. As party-goers imbibe from these pilfered vessels – praising the gods of gold, silver, bronze, iron and wood – the fingers of a human hand appear opposite a lamp-stand and begin writing on the plaster wall of the palace.

Belshazzar's complexion turns chalky, and his hip joints and knees start to wobble as the disembodied hand writes an undecipherable inscription for all to see. Daniel is summoned to translate the missive which reads: *Mene, Tekel, Peres*...King Belshazzar's days are numbered. He had been "weighed on the scales and found wanting, and his kingdom will be divided." (Daniel 5: 25). In fact the number of days left would turn out to be less than one. "That very night Belshazzar, the Chaldean king, was slain." (Daniel 5:30).

Few of us ever get instructions as clear as handwriting on the wall. In the situation described above, the word "DO" on my bedroom wall resulted from a motion sensor tripping a light over the garage of a nearby house and sending its beams through the circular vents of a window-mounted air conditioner in our bedroom. Instead of two circles of light, a pole lamp in front of one of the vents changed one circle into a "D" resulting in a glowing word across from the bed. Secular humanists and concrete thinkers of every ilk are satisfied with this rational and completely scientific explanation as just another manifestation of natural law without a need to examine any deeper significance.

Janet Richards

The more mystical among us wonder, as my friend Gerard stated with a confident smile, "That happened for a reason."

Primo Levi might beg to differ. As a prisoner in a concentration camp for eleven months during World War II, he witnessed the Nazi's arbitrary evaluation of captives bound for Auschwitz initially on the basis of their age, health, and presumed abilities to work for the Reich. But this was not always the case. Levi writes:

> We also know that not even this tenuous principle of discrimination between fit and unfit was always followed, and that later the simpler method was often adopted of merely opening both the doors of the wagon without warning or instructions to the new arrivals. Those who by chance climbed down on one side of the convoy entered the camp; the others went to the gas chamber.

Questions about divine providence will not let me go. How does one make peace with the idea of chance, luck, and apparent randomness of adversity when a crazed shooter fires into a crowd? How do we reconcile tsunamis that sweep away hundreds of thousands or the flimsy hold on life of those precious souls who simply exited the Nazi train on the wrong side, with a God who cares and directs and guides his creatures.

Christopher Page writes in his blog *In a Spacious Place, Reflections on the Journey in Christ*:

> There are times in the unfolding human drama when it feels as if God has abandoned the stage, leaving the human community to blunder unaided through a cold dark meaningless abyss. Life feels completely random and chaotic. We can find no way to discern any meaning, pattern,

or purpose in the midst of the disordered horror that seems to be the only reality.

Later Page offers:

> Providence is not a divine Puppet Master in the sky pulling the strings in favor of those he chooses. Providence is the consciousness that, deeper than the pain and horror, there are forces at work in the universe that are always tending towards light and nurturing the possibility of life. Against all odds in the depths of night, the dawn still stirs. This is the force we call 'Providence'.

And he concludes his essay with a quote from Jacques Lusseyran, *And There Was Light: Autobiography of Jacques Lusseyran: Blind Hero of the French Resistance.* (trans. Elizabeth R. Cameron. NY: Parabola Books, 1963, 282.) "...joy does not come from outside, for whatever happens to us it is within...light does not come to us from without. Light is in us, even if we have no eyes. And we can trust this light for it is Jesus."

Whether an agent of God was spurring me to action or not, Natalie's suggestion moves me. The next day I'm on the road to Monty's grandma's house on the Key Peninsula. Once again I am headed for Home.

## Chapter 22

> "There comes a moment to everyone
> When Beauty stands staring into the soul
> with sad, sweet eyes
> That sicken at the sound of words,
> And God help those who pass that
> moment by."
>
> — Cyrano

Monty's dumpy canned ham haven lies fallow in the tall grass behind his grandma's house. The tiny anteroom by the front door of her home that once held a computer desk and little else now serves as a makeshift sick room. All treatment options have been exhausted. Monty is home on hospice.

It's early September, and the leaves are just starting to turn – there's a slight chill in the air. Yvonne's house has undergone some renovations and looks better than ever. Dad, Boone, Daniel, and friends worked for weeks to make repairs – replace a leaky roof and install new flooring, sheetrock, and molding with funds from a special program at Seattle Children's

Hospital. Monty's space is freshly painted and has two small windows. Lisa hung curtains.

Friends and family come and go at Yvonne's place, which is a marked improvement over the isolation of the cancer center but a liability when it comes to privacy. Monty spends most of every day in a rented hospital bed crammed catty-cornered into the entryway along with a tray-table and commode chair. His bed faces the front door, and the portable toilet blocks the narrow passage to the kitchen and living area. He's sitting on the portable potty when I step to the entrance and knock. I can see him through the screen door.

"Hi, Mrs. Richards," he states flatly, in his usual matter-of-fact manner. "Come in."

A newly purchased flat screen television wedged into the corner plays a movie full blast, and canned laughter peels from another set in the living room where Yvonne's watching a game show. The inside air smells of a mixture of cigarette smoke and cooked coffee. Lisa works hard, and everything is neat and tidy except for the clutter on the table by the bed. She runs out from the kitchen to give me a hug. It's like we never parted.

"I'm sorry about this," Monty says, gesturing toward the portable toilet and his bare chest. His trunk is swathed in blankets, and the commode is barely visible under yards of fabric.

"I'll come back later," I say, aware of how modest he's always been. How hard it must be for someone his age to be so vulnerable.

"It's okay for you stay if it doesn't bother you, Mrs. Richards," he says without an ounce of embarrassment.

"I'm a nurse Monty."

I make a conscious effort not to show my shock at the changes in the young man's appearance. Monty's ragged goatee is dotted with crumbs from his last meal, and his once beautiful golden blond hair looks like a matted nest of dusky curls that, by his own admission, have turned "the color of scummy pond water."

His normally sharp facial features are puffy and distorted, and crescent-shaped rolls of fat cascade under his chin. The cancer is crimping his spinal cord and crowding his internal organs, compromising his circulation and causing his bloated abdomen to bulge like a giant water balloon. The skin on his remaining leg is shiny and taut—a boggy log of a leg. It's entirely possible that Monty's weight has more than doubled in just a matter of months.

He can't use his right arm at all now, and his left one is barely functioning. He's paralyzed and unable to feel anything below his upper chest. Weeks of radiation treatment at the University of Washington specifically designed to clear the tumor from his spinal cord, at least temporarily and improve the quality of his remaining days of life seem to have been futile. A plastic bag of IV fluid hangs on a short pole at the bedside feeding a continuous drip of the narcotic into Monty's bloodstream via his port to help lessen any pain from the tumor's invasion into his upper spine. Despite the seriousness of his situation, he only mentions his disabilities in one brief comment in passing.

"I'm sort of stuck here, Mrs. Richards. Can't get up, and can't move any part of my body except my left arm. It's a good thing I'm left handed."

Yvonne often smokes in a chair behind the half wall that separates Monty's bedroom from her tiny living room only a few feet away. Lisa is a caring, attentive nurse. Boone supplies daily breakfasts and dinners from the diner down the road. A Franciscan Hospice volunteer has become a friend and confidant, and a nurse comes check on the patient at least once a week.

Lisa and I work to remove the turban of blankets and transfer Monty's hefty immobile form, clad only in Depends and a t-shirt, back into bed. The difficult move from portable toilet to bed and back takes time. It's no wonder he hasn't gone farther than a trip to and from the bedside commode for weeks. We drape him in a flannel blue and red patchwork lap robe I made years ago.

"I'm so glad you are using this quilt, Mont. I know it's not your style but I wanted you to have it so that you can feel my love across the miles," I comment in one of my rare lapses into sappy sentimentality. "It's one of my 'gypsy' creations."

A similar blanket made its way to a small rural village in Ukraine when my daughter, Noelle, was in the Peace Corps. Her host family gave the quilt a gypsy moniker, unaware that our family jokes of a possible genetic connection to the gypsies because of my Austrian grandmother's unknown paternity.

"I like it, Mrs. Richards," he says stroking the fabric. "I use it all the time."

Once settled and tucked in, Monty eyes a box of bacon covered maple bars on his bedside table with frank desire.

"Did you bring those for me?"

"They are something new – bacon on a donut, a nice sugar and fat combo. I heard you're hungry and are into carbs."

"They have me on the steroids, Mrs. Richards."

I love to see the glint in my boy's eyes as he stretches out his good hand to gingerly pick up a maple bar. He takes his time with it, as if to extract every bite of sugary goodness, nibbling his way through the treat with the studied care of a Zen master before helping himself to another. Even at the age of eight, I noticed a tenacious perfectionism in Monty that I admired – a stick-to-it kind of attitude that helped him forge ahead. This was the personality trait that gave him the persistence to craft crude machines from cardboard using intricate step-by-step instructions, insist on untangling a messy clump of fishing line caught in the weeds instead of just cutting it loose, and later to rescue an injured horse and diligently clean its wounds. I always thought that with his love of animals and the right environment, financing, and encouragement he could have been a veterinary surgeon. Instead he channeled his perfectionism into his work as a sheet metal artist.

Once done with the donuts, Monty turns to a Styrofoam box his Dad left on the tray table and begins to carefully prepare his next course – a stack of dinner plate-sized flapjacks smothered with more than a half a cup of syrup. He slowly and patiently devours them, carefully sopping up every drop of mapley goodness with the careful attention of someone savoring an expensive glass of wine.

Monty dozes after this mega meal. TV's blare at both ends of the house, and I quietly reach for the remote to turn down the sound of the horror show playing on the one next to the bed. A crazed character who looks like Jack Nicholson in the movie the *Shining* hacks a woman to pieces with a machete. Virtual blood spurts. Simulated body parts and chunks of flesh fly through the air.

"How can you stomach these gory flicks, Monty?" I ask later in the day, sounding like the clueless elderly curmudgeon I've become. "Is there really an audience for this kind movie – flesh ripping, blood dripping? Yuck, Mont. It's horrible. Why do you watch this stuff?"

"It's makes you face what scares you, Mrs. Richards. That's why it's so popular."

"That sounds like something from the bible –'Don't fear what a man can do to your body'."

"Huh?"

"Yes. 'But be afraid of the one who can destroy your soul'."

Monty looks serious. Lisa bought him the movie *Heaven is for Real,* and he's been watching it. We've had some serious discussions about hope and heaven.

"Hope and heaven, Mrs. Richards. I can only hope that heaven is for real," he says with a smile.

I say no more. Logic and sermons never convince. "The damp of the night drives deeper into the soul," says Walt Whitman. This I know is true.

The hours of this day by Monty's bedside unfold and fall like pleats fanning into the pages of the past. Afternoon begins to fade into early evening, and, when he's awake, we stay in the moment, nattering on about the usual mundane stuff. At some point he begins reminiscing about the natural beauty of the Key peninsula, and his desire to be outside. Even though it's close to 6 p.m., the idea of a walk seems good and right, and we decide to try to head out for a spin.

Lisa pulls a pair of shorts over Monty's *Depends,* and Boone maneuvers his boy's leaden frame into a wheelchair with a sliding board. I ease the wobbly wheels over the threshold and bump down a makeshift ramp hobbled together from sheets of paneling. The rickety rental chair creaks with Monty's weight as it teeters across the gravel driveway. We're heading toward the one and only restaurant in Home at the end of Carr's Inlet without a clue to the difficulties we might be facing.

Noble firs and cedars tower over the paved path ahead, bending their needled boughs to embrace us as we lumber forward. Twilight is just beginning to spreads its golden haze. A cool breeze, infused with balsam, caresses our faces with unexpected gentleness. We both tip our heads back for a draw of its grace. Faint rays of sun flicker through the dusky thicket, and bright strips of light paint the aisle of this natural cathedral as Venus rises to begin evening vespers. The woods are silent – no organ or choir in this sanctuary. We're headed to Lulu's where a table waits – the cup, the bread – communion served on paper placemats.

Ever so slowly Monty and I make our way along narrow asphalt lanes, wheels crunching over a needled carpet that pads our way up gentle hills and softly down again. A bird skitters through the evergreen boughs oblivious to the strange twosome plowing along this rural road – a pudgy middle aged woman – red faced, arms extended, pushing a very swollen man with a urinary catheter bag hidden in his Grandma's black plastic handbag hanging on his neck.

The route is undulating and pavement uneven. I use my legs to bulldoze up inclines and brake hard on steep downslopes sprinkled with pea gravel that acts like greased ball bearings. My hands ache and my arms tremble and strain as I labor to keep the wheelchair straight. It takes on momentum with Monty's bulky weight and lists with the slope of the road toward a deep ditch and certain disaster. Monty and I both feel anxious. I try not to imagine what would happen if he tipped into the trench.

We make it to the flat plane of a two-lane highway and stop on the shoulder for a rest. Monty suggests we visit his friend Jerry at his trailer by a former convenience store down the road. Jerry has an expensive bottle of Monk's Ale, which Monty has been dreaming about for some time.

"His place is right on the way Mrs. Richards. This ale is supposed to be the best in the world, and Jerry owes me big time."

We spy Jerry's trailer from the highway, and I jostle the chair across a strip of rocky hard-pan onto a dirt trail at the bottom of a hill. The wheels of Monty's feeble chair sink into the soft sandy soil at the foot of the steep incline we have to climb to get to the bank of trailers at the top.

"We won't make it up there, Monty. I don't think I'm strong enough. This chair is about to fall apart."

"It's Monks Ale, Mrs. Richards. It's $14 a bottle. It's liquid gold. The monks know what they are doing. They've been brewing this stuff for thousands of years."

"Thousands of years....? Come on Monty, that isn't true."

"It's an ancient recipe."

"And I'm feeling as old as that recipe, Mont. It's crazy to try and get up there. What if the chair blows apart or starts rolling backwards and I can't stop it?"

Monty ignores me and commences to expound on the virtues of Monk's Ale. He argues as only Monty can offering specifics of the special brewing process, quality ingredients, and all the taste sensations offered by this particular brand of beer, and as always, embellishing his pitch with impassioned assurance of the absolute truth of his information..

"It's brewed by friars on the grounds of a Benedictine

Monastery, Mrs. Richards. No outsiders can enter the abbey. It's rare to even find a bottle in this state."

As with so many of Monty's lengthy soliloquies on various subjects, I'm not sold. The supposed "rarity" is a large part of the ale's appeal, but it's probably available in any specialty store that carries swanky brews. I'm out of shape and sure that one bottle of beer, no matter how "amazing", is not worth the pain I am about to experience or the risk of an accidental tip-over or an involuntary roll-back. But, once again, I cut some slack. Somehow I summon the courage to try.

Our ascent to the top of Jerry's driveway defies reason. All four limbs burn as I soldier up the precipitous slope a few inches at a time bracing my feet with every step to keep the wheels from rolling backward and sending us both flying down the slope. Monty tries to help, but his only functional arm lacks strength. Ever so slowly, with Monty's verbal encouragement, I plow up the hill, eyes on the goal, until, much to my immense relief, I manage to move the massive bulk of my friend, his chair, and my aged body onto level ground and crunch down the pebbly driveway to the front door of the trailer. I'm so thankful that Jerry's home to answer the door.

The three of us stay in the driveway just chatting away as night falls. Jerry's a tall skinny guy with the weathered look of someone who's been around the block a few times, and he obviously likes to gab. Everyone's talking about a local yokel's hash oil manufacturing mishap which landed him in a burn unit in Seattle, and Jerry clues us in on recent developments. A spate of break-ins on the Key Peninsula, the state of the Lakebay Post Office, and Jerry's long-term girlfriend's health are just a few of the matters he covers at length. It takes the better part of an hour just to catch up on the news of Monty's friend's financial and relational woes, employment issues, and his hopes for the future. If Jerry's surprised by the changes in Monty's appearance, he doesn't let on. The topic of cancer never comes up.

It's almost dark, and there's a chill in the air when we finally say goodbye to Jerry. The bottle of ale, when it finally appears from inside the defunct store next to the trailer, is non-descript – a small brown bottle with a label depicting a stained glass window and the silhouette of several monks facing a golden cross. But it is pure joy for Monty, an alabaster cruse of spikenard, which Jerry offers with open hands.

Monty accepts the coveted bottle with profuse thanks and nestles it in the purse next to his urine bag, where it's safely buffered for the harrowing slide down the dirt footpath toward the highway. I find that the downslope is easier to navigate with both handbrakes partially engaged to buffer the movement of the wheels. The extra pounds I carry come in handy for deceleration, and we make it to the flat asphalt roadway without incident. Cars whiz by with headlights beaming as the two of us rumble along on the tight shoulder and push ahead toward the lights of the diner and nearby Shell Station in the distance.

Lulu's Homeport is a small establishment with all the personality of a small town cafe – sagging vinyl booths, greasy paper menus, walls covered with fake wood paneling and paintings of weathered cowboys done by a local hobbyist. A blast of hot air and the unmistakable aroma of stale beer, grilled burgers, and potatoes frying in deep fat hits when I push open the glass door and struggle to maneuver the wheelchair inside. George Strait croons "Give It All We Got Tonight" from speakers in a murky bar behind a beaded curtain at the back of the building. A stocky cook in a sweatshirt with the sleeves rolled up waves and greets Monty by name through a slit in the wall behind a long counter lined with metal stools. A teenage waitress in a tight t-shirt and torn Levis comes over to chat. Monty knows everyone in this place. Grandma, Boone, and Lisa have worked here for years.

The two of us find a small table by the front that has room for the wheelchair and order a Reuben sandwich, a juicy cheeseburger, and two large sides of fries. We dip crispy potato wedges into a mound of ketchup, relishing each salty, savory bite and agree, "This is good food." Other customers come and go, and the waitress continues to refill our drinks, but Monty and I are in no hurry. It's close to ten when we decide to venture out into the dark and head back toward Yvonne's house.

The air is even cooler now, and the briny smell of ocean is welcome after hours inhaling the odor of stale beer and the smoky smell of fatty beef sizzling on a grille. The sky over Tacoma glows orange in the distance, tinting the heavens with a mysterious radiance. A few bright orbs dapple the darkness closer to Home. No cars are out tonight.

Once we navigate the speed bumps in the Country Store parking lot next door to the restaurant and hustle past the gas pump Monty once decimated, we hit the smooth pavement of a narrow strip of road along the Carr Inlet. We stroll past fancy summer houses with vegetable gardens and pergolas overlooking the water. We spy the sandy bar across the bridge on the other side of the inlet where Monty and I explored one long afternoon on my visit almost nine years ago—a special day when it seemed like we had all the time in the world.

A motor boat of partiers chugs by and Monty calls out to them.

"How's it going? Catch anything?" Monty hollers without a hint of the sadness in his voice. He is just being Monty.

The tipsy boaters shout their hellos, raise beer bottles in toast, and speed onward. I doubt that they are fishing, but it feels so good to be normal – to be out in the world and back into the stream of living with others who are enjoying this beautiful evening. It feels good to connect.

Eventually the chair rolls to a stop under a single street light at the foot of a hill that's too steep to scale. Liquid light streams from the lamp overhead like a spotlight on a stage, its rays falling like strands of neon into a shaft of golden tinsel all the brighter against the a moonless velvet sky peppered with stars. Monty and I bend toward it. We bask in the street lamp's offering as if warmed by the breath of an unseen God. When I look at my boy he seems to glow.

"From time to time during our earthly journey, we may glimpse at the edge of perception, the radiant beauty of another's soul in the blinding flash of a light." Peggy Wilkinson calls this a "transfiguration experience." In a moment like this, "divinity smiles out at us from other eyes...and its significance can neither be mistaken nor denied."

Monty and I wait under the light of this street lamp for some time – just two souls, a grotesquely bloated, desperately sick young man with a trusty companion at his side. I've driven across the state of Washington to push him through the cedars on this summer night, and there is no other place in the universe that I would rather be.

I joy in this memory. I ponder it with true wonder as I do so many others – eight-year-old Monty lighting our candle, searching the internet for advice on how to nurse a broken bird back to health, and the two of us scraping ice crystals off his mother grave stone with our bare hands on a frigid morning in February.

I see Monty smiling and giving me the thumbs up through the mirror in the MRI room as I watch him slide into the giant machine from my post in the corner while tamping my earplugs with both thumbs. I hear Monty chattering on and on about Nikoli Tesla, the *Bronies* and *My Little Pony* characters, and tormenting Jesse with a relentless series of details about Mr. Rogers' sweaters and gnarly tattoos.

I remember him showing me the crazy inventions he'd crafted from hospital trash to pass the time and make things more bearable for himself and perhaps other cancer patients isolated in sterile rooms with the incessant high pitched beeping of alarms and nowhere to turn.

I hold onto the delight in his eyes as he showed me how to use the remote to control lights outlining the ceiling of his room in the brand new cancer ward.

"I like green during the day and change it to blue at night," he explained, as he flicked a button on the remote – a scant instance of power in a powerless place.

But most of all, I think of how he told me of his desire to make his mark on the world, and how he felt he hadn't done that.

Memories of these times together are burned into my heart. Like his mother Heather's love for her children, they are eternal and will never be taken away.

"Remember when I walked across the roof of the snow cave and buried Neal and his friends?" he asks as we wait under the streetlamp for Boone to pick us up.

"Those guys are still talking about that, Monty. You got them good and they were sure upset."

"Remember when that bear cub ran in front of the van on our way back from fishing at Cottonwood?"

"That bear climbed up a tree so fast, if I recall. We never saw its mother."

"Remember when I dressed Pneuma in the cheerleader's costume?"

"I do remember, Monty. Pneuma was a special dog and such a snuggle-pup. She was good to let you dress her up, because not too many of the canine species will allow that kind of humiliation. It was so sad when she was lost in the desert. I still miss her."

"...and when I dropped one of the sheep in the nativity set on the fireplace and broke all its legs off, and we glued them back on?"

"You were only eight years old when that happened, Mont, and I couldn't believe that you told me that lamb symbolized Jesus, broken for us. I think you learned that when you went to the Awana program at the Baptist church."

"I took myself there, Mrs. Richards. I walked there on my own every Wednesday night."

"You know we still have that lamb. The Superglue on its legs still holds. It's part of the nativity we set up every year. I think about you every time I pick it up,"

"Remember when Tom took me out into the garage to teach me how to sharpen a can opener?"

"What?"

"That's the main memory I have of Tom."

"How to sharpen a can opener...? How strange..."

"Not too useful."

Monty smiles and I smile with him. We laugh at the power of seemingly insignificant things and moments – the absurdity of life. We laugh and the sound of our laughter fills the night as we huddle together under the light of the lamp.

And laughing feels so good. Like a phoenix rising. It echoes into the heavens.

And something true and good sprang forth in this spontaneous mirth – a glimpse of the sacred that so often comes in the most unexpected places. It begins to sparkle and shine through the horrors that have overtaken my beloved boy, my Godson.

Even in the face of the evil that abounds in this worldly life, seemingly so arbitrary and unfair, the good triumphs.

The darkness is powerless to overcome its brilliance.

## Chapter 23

> "To everything there is a season;
> A time to be born and a time to die.
> A time to plant and a time for harvest.
> A time to meet and a time to part."
>
> — M. D. Ridge, a parable
> Refrain #1 and 4
> Based on Ecclesiates 3: 1-9

I'm awake early on the morning of September 12th. A digital clock on a bedside table reads 5:15 a.m. My husband and I are staying with our friends, Jeff and Julie, in their home off the grid in the mountains south of Lakeview. The house is silent and crisp, piney air wafts through an open window in our upstairs room. I can see the tops of the giant ponderosas outside from second floor, their boughs arching toward a cloudless sky, and hear birds warbling in the junipers surrounding the cabin. It looks to be Rocky Mountain High kind of day.

My heart races as I ponder our plans for the hours ahead. I haven't been entirely honest with my husband and there's no way I can drift back to sleep. I lured him to our friend's Southern

Oregon get-away on the pretense of attending our friend Bill's sixty-fifth birthday party, which our friends all celebrated the previous evening. Today is the day my three children and their families will be gathering in Bend to surprise my husband with the real reason for the trip south – a weekend retreat with kids and grandkids in a rented ranch house in the Steens Mountains in the southeast corner of Oregon. Anticipation of my husband's shock and my glee at pulling off the ruse has me feeling giddy. Tom's always been so sure he can "read me like a book." He's a medical professional, after all, and used to noticing every little detail and nuance, and I have an expressive face to boot. Everyone in the family (including me) has been surprised at the success of our plans so far.

Thoughts of Monty drift into my mind as I lay on my back gazing upward at the towering trees. He received a letter inviting him to read his story, "The Love of One Man," at a writer's event scheduled for the end of September. He wrote the piece in conjunction with the *Writers in Schools Program* of Seattle Arts and Lectures at Seattle Children's, and it was included it in an anthology entitled *The Sixth Breath Blows You Home*. Daniel reported that Monty was seeing visions of his mother and other relatives who'd passed away (a common experience for those near death), and I worried that he wouldn't feel well enough or even be alive to attend the reading. I planned to head to the Key Peninsula after our weekend get-together in just five days. I would tell Monty about how we duped Tom. He would love hearing about that.

Without warning an image of Jesus enters my mind's eye. Not an actual, embodied person, but a picture of the face of the traditional bearded Christ as if projected on a screen. His face and hair are all light, and he is smiling. He looks at me with kind eyes. He winks.

This mental impression is gone in a flash, and I instantly dismiss it as a product of an overactive imagination or even a waking dream and don't give it another thought. Mystical experiences are generally attributed to the saints in legends of extraordinary devotion, not something I or anyone I know ever experience first-hand.

Tom and I eventually get up to enjoy a leisurely breakfast with our host and hostess. We pack our bags, say our goodbyes, drive down the mountain on a washboard dirt incline, ford Davis Creek, and head to the highway that leads toward Lakeview.

The news arrives via text as we finally come into range for cell service. Monty died shortly after 5:15 that morning. Lisa later reported that at the moment of death her stepson shouted, "UP, UP, UP."

She thought Monty was calling for her to raise the head of his bed.

That may be true.

Or maybe not.

# Chapter 24

I made a trip back to the Key Peninsula several weeks after Monty's death. I went to see Boone and Lisa and give them framed photos of their son. We hugged each other like there was no tomorrow. We are family now.

The pictures I brought had been taken and compiled into a book by a couple who took Monty into their home during his high school years. I never heard if his friends had a memorial service although I hope they planned some kind of event to mark his passing. Enlarging and framing the pictures became one way for me to honor Monty's life.

"I'm giving these to you, Mrs. Richards," he said during that day we spent talking in his trailer. "I know you will take care of them."

I was humbled by his trust in me.

Lisa and I talk on the phone every once in a while. Shortly after Monty passed, Yvonne was diagnosed with cancer and joined her grandson. I still keep in touch with Chris. She lives in Lakeview with her daughter and continues to struggle with health issues. Daniel and Boone are reportedly doing well. Jesse and I have spoken a couple of times. He's moved on with his life.

Years after my last visit to Home the phone rang. It was my friend from St. Vincent De Paul (SVDP) asking me to contact a gentleman who called our hotline to request help paying for his medications. SVDP is a lay ministry of the Catholic Church, which is available to assist people in emergency situations with rent, utilities, and a wide variety of other needs. Our members visit with people who request assistance to determine the best way to help. I headed out to meet the client at a local clinic.

"Tell me about your life, Randy, I asked, as we sat by the pharmacy window waiting for his prescription to be filled.

We soon learn that Randy and I have several things in common. We are both parents of three children, two girls and a boy. He spent time in a transitional housing program where I worked as a receptionist several years ago. Randy once stayed in a Ronald McDonald House while his daughter underwent treatment for leukemia.

"What hospital was she in, I asked.

"Katie was in the Children's Hospital in Seattle."

"Yikes, Randy, I stayed at the Ronald McDonald House in Seattle too – the big building on 40$^{th}$ Avenue right by the Metro Market and the Burke-Gilman Trail."

"When was that?" he asked.

"The last time was about three years ago. My friend Monty stayed there while he had chemotherapy for bone cancer."

"How old was he?"

"He was nineteen when he was diagnosed with osteosarcoma, which is considered a childhood cancer. The doctors had been treating him for a sports injury because of his age, and the cancer went too long without treatment."

"Did he have his leg amputated?"

"Yes...his left leg above the knee."

"I knew him. We played basketball and computer games. I even remember the game we used to play, 'Plants versus the Zombies.' He had a lot of pain but hated to take pain medicine."

"He was a remarkable person, Randy.
"I sensed that."
"I can't believe he touched your life, too."
"God works in mysterious ways, doesn't He, Janet?"
"Yes He does. Yes He does."

# *Epilogue*

*"A shadow owes its birth to light."*

— John Gray (poet and dramatist)

Monty played the hand he was dealt. He didn't fold despite being given a life that included the diagnosis of "stupid cancer" at age nineteen. He didn't opt for poison hemlock or a lethal dose of one of the modern pharmaceuticals to avoid the emotional and physical pain, paralysis, and dependency that ensued when medical science had run out of options. He said yes to life and life kept offering some joy in a variety of ways that no one, not even him, could have imagined.

Friends in and near Home rallied around to throw a party in his honor, and people stopped by daily to share themselves and their resources. Chris got to visit one last time and other family members and visitors had a chance to show him how much he meant to them. Lisa borrowed an electric wheelchair for a trip to the casino where Monty won $1,000 playing the slots. He rode a speed boat and Ferris wheel and had deep conversations with his Franciscan Hospice worker. He reconciled with Jesse.

The movie *Yes Man* is about a guy who stumbles upon

a way out of his post-divorce depression by buying into the message of a guru at a motivational seminar, who insists that his followers say "yes" to every opportunity that comes along. The covenant of "yes" connects the main character, Carl (played by Jim Carey), to a host of new adventures – flight lessons, second language classes, relationships and a romance that he would have missed if he'd continued playing video games in his apartment after work every night. Carl begrudgingly says "yes" to a homeless man's request for a ride and money, which in time leads to an encounter with the woman of his dreams. Choosing to answer "yes" to every question presented, despite his fear and reluctance to take chances, took the protagonist of this film to places and experiences he never envisioned. Of course, there came a time when a firm "no" became necessary, but only after weighing the facts.

Who has all the facts about the meaning of life? Who knows what purpose lies beyond all we see and know? What if we don't have enough information to make the decision to say "no" to living. What if we don't know what we are losing?

What if what the Bible says is true – that "a day is like a thousand years, and a thousand years are like a day" (Peter 3:8), and every second and every moment of every life contains a hidden gift that keeps on giving – an open-ended chance for an unimagined splendor, something to be cherished. What if what Milton wrote in 1667 is true, that this life is only a shadow of the one to come and that "each to other life, is more than on earth is thought?"

John Steinbeck's momentous novel *East of Eden* tells the story of humans caught in an epic struggle. "Was your life good or was it evil?" the narrator asks. He tells of the death of a man who enabled others to experience dignity when the whole world seemed to want to tear them down and make them cower in their fears. When that man died, the people burst into tears in the streets, and their minds wailed, "What can we do now? How can we go on without him?" Father M. Gula once wrote in the March 11, 2016 edition of *This Day* "The measure of a life well lived is the virtue that continues to grow in the lives of those who were touched by it."

From his place of dying, Monty gifted me with something precious – a clear example of human virtue and courage and a glimpse into the holiness and beauty that suffering can produce in the sufferer.

Maybe Monty has gifted you too. If you have gotten to this point in the book, his story has become part of yours. Perhaps Monty's example has given you courage to say yes in the face of seemingly insurmountable odds.

If even one more soul in this vast world of ours sees the beauty and dignity in this man's journey and is encouraged and inspired to go on and face whatever life brings, it will mean so much.

In fact, this has already happened.

Monty Martin McDonald, you have made your mark.

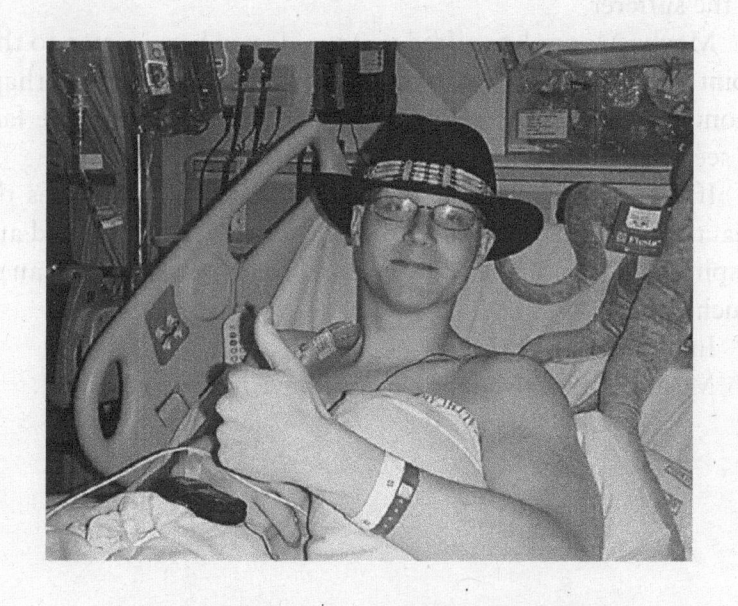

*"Life seems more sweet that thou didst live
And men more true that thou wert one
Nothing is lost that thou didst give
Nothing destroyed that thou has done."*

— Anne Bronte

- Thank you Will Cahill for having the heart to recognize Daniel's need for special attention after his mother's death. If you hadn't thought to send Monty's brother to the middle school library for some TLC, this book might never have been written. Whenever one person shows respect for another person, God is there.
- Thank you Christine for all you did to nurture and protect your brothers over the years. I am in awe of your strength and the woman you have become through all the trials you have faced.
- Thank you Daniel for the deep love you communicated to your brother. You were the first person he thought about after learning that his leg would be amputated. Monty truly loved you, and I think that, more than anything, he wanted you to be well and happy. May you honor Monty by living a virtuous life and passing the love he showed you to others who cross your path.
- Thank you Lisa for the compassion you showed to your boy during his last days on earth. Your tender touch, sensitive nature, and energetic presence were a blessing to your stepson. These are the best gifts anyone can give to another person.
- Thank you Boone for loving Monty unconditionally. Monty was eight years old when I met you at Hunter's Hot Springs, and I will never forget how your eyes lit up when he ran to you. I felt your joy in him then, and, years later, your overwhelming grief at his passing. My hope is that this book will bring you comfort.
- Thank you, Jesse, for stepping up when no one else could or would. No greater love has a man than to lay down his life for a friend. You are a hero in my eyes, Jesse, and you always will be.
- Thank you Dr. Conrad for caring for Monty and trying to save his life. I know you gave your best.

- And finally thank you Dr. Lux for your extraordinary words of compassion. May you always know the power of offering yourself.

"A single sunbeam is enough to drive away many shadows."
(St. Francis of Assissi)

# The Love of One Man
## By Monty McDonald

I had a horse named Luna. She was a very nice horse. She had a terrible accident in her life. At the dude ranch where she lived they had their own private trails in back. Horses could travel on them so the guides would know where a horse was if it didn't come back. Luna was learning how to be the leader, and some people were four-wheeling on the path and went off a bump and went right in her face!

The owners wrapped bandages all around her so she wouldn't lose much blood. They were about to kill her, just kill her, because she was in so much misery, but the horse doctor asked to be able to try something. They put her in a special front part of a harness with pieces of strong rubber to transport her.

The vet did a great job reconstructing Luna's face, but they asked the dentist to work on her tooth – [stuff] kept draining and was coming out of her face. The dentist jammed a rubber hose tube in there so it could just drain out. But no one was cleaning it. It was hanging off her face. After they got her back, she couldn't canter anymore, which is what people visiting the ranch wanted. I decided that I would buy her and take care of her. But, when I got to the dude ranch, they told me they already sold her to a dog food processing plant. So I floored it, did 90 to get there.

Do you know what animals I saw there? I saw an alpaca with a giant tumor on its neck, pigs with so many flies it looked like their skin was rotting off, a couple of peacocks. I was able to buy Luna for a couple hundred dollars.

The very first thing I did was clear the giant amount of [drainage] off her face. I cleaned out the inside of her wound with a Q-tip and eventually the outpour stopped. And I rubbed Vaseline on her wounds. I treated her almost every day. And Luna would pack hay into her cheeks, maybe because of the pain, packing it way up there. Which seemed okay at first, but then seemed like it was getting moldy, so I reached back in and pulled it all out. It was every stripe of green from fresh grass all the way down to a gray slimy layer. I had to take care of that, too.

I used to ride her, but I got too big for her. She was half Tennessee Walker and half Quarter Horse. But we had a friend who had a little kid, who was just the right size for this horse. So I gave them Luna for their kid, even though I loved that horse a bunch.

A month later they seemed to be doing everything to take care of her. But a couple of months later I stopped by and learned that all three of them were gone, though they had a friend who was supposed to be taking care of the animals. But Luna's wounds looked bad, so obviously he didn't.

I hopped the fence and got her cleaned up again. Just as I hopped back out the family actually was pulling in, back from the trip. It was pretty funny.

And all this coming from a one-legged kid with a half paralyzed spine

# Works Cited

Collins, Billy. *Poetry 180: A Turning Back to Poetry*. New York: Random House Trade Paperbacks, 2003. Print. Pages 231-232

Levi, Primo (Author). "If This Is a Man and The Truce (Penguin Modern Classics) Hardcover – June, 1979." *If This Is a Man and The Truce (Penguin Modern Classics): Primo Levi: 9780140047233: Amazon.com: Books*. N.p., n.d. Web. 29 July 2017. page 26

Lusseyran, Jacques, and Elizabeth R. Cameron. *And There Was Light: The Extraordinary Memoir of a Blind Hero of the French Resistance in World War II*. NY: Parabola, 1963. Print. page 312

*The New American Bible*. New York, NY: Oxford UP, 2004. Print.

Nouwen, Henri J. M. *Behold the Beauty of the Lord: Praying with Icons*. Notre Dame, IN: Ave Maria, 2007. Print. Page 20-22

Page, Christopher. "In A Spacious Place." *Providence*. N.p., n.d. Web. 29 July 2017.

Peterson, Eugene H. *A Long Obedience in the Same Direction: Discipleship in an Instant Society.* Downers Grove, IL: InterVarsity, 2000. Print.

Rosenthal, Amy Krouse. "You May Want to Marry My Husband (Updated With Podcast)." *The New York Times.* The New York Times, 03 Mar. 2017. Web. 29 July 2017.

Wilkinson (Author), Peggy. Washington DC: ICS Publications, 1999. Print. page 72